SOCCER SHORTS

Jack Rollin

GUINNESS BOOKS

Editor: Honor Head
Design and Layout: Michael Morey

© Jack Rollin and Guinness Publishing Ltd, 1988

Published in Great Britain by Guinness Publishing Ltd,
33 London Road, Enfield, Middlesex

Typeset in Garamond Light 8/9
by Ace Filmsetting Ltd, Frome, Somserset
Printed and bound in Great Britain by The Bath Press, Bath

'Guinness' is a registered trade mark of Guinness Superlatives Ltd

British Library Cataloguing in Publication Data
Rollin, Jack,
    Guinness soccer shorts.
    1. Great Britain. Association football
    I. Title
    796.334'0941

    ISBN 0-85112-321-X

GUINNESS BOOKS

SOCCER SHORTS

Jack Rollin is seen above as a 14-year-old in 1946 shortly after being offered a trial with *Chicago Maroons* who had been beaten 9–3 by Liverpool on their USA tour. He later switched to goalkeeping when Leon Greene (opera singer, actor and film star) became unavailable – and stayed between the posts.

Learning to play the piano at five years of age, Jack won a certificate of merit at six and now cannot play a note. Similar loss of faculty occurred with shorthand, Jack having at one time scribbled at 150 wpm when he first became a journalist, to completely ruin his handwriting. Thankfully for his editors he can still touch-type.

Three-and-a-half years in the RAF included such wide-ranging duties as guarding Queen Juliana of the Netherlands and acting as Officers Mess Librarian at Fighter Command HQ, but chiefly involved playing a lot of football, cricket and tennis.

Jack retains fond memories of growing-up pastimes: train spotting, smoking cinnamon sticks, munching at the school tuck shop, collecting cigarette cards and swing records, going to the cinema and sitting in 'The Gods', reading *Stars and Stripes* and listening to *Children's Hour* and *Dick Barton* while doing his homework.

Jack Rollin would like to thank Christine Phillips for all her work in collating the material for this book.

Cover design: David Roberts
Cover artwork: Rob Burns
Cartoons: Dan Donovan

CONTENTS

This book is dedicated
to
"Dill and Josie"

IN THE BEGINNING

At the start of the 1950–51 season all the promoted teams lost on the first day, all the relegated sides won and the newly-elected clubs drew.

Inside-forward Bill Horton's first three appearances in first-class football were made in three different national competitions with Aldershot: the FA Cup in 1961–62 and the Football League Cup and the Football League in that order in 1962–63.

Queen's Park claim to have been the first Scottish club to appear on television, the first to install x-ray equipment and the first to introduce a 3 pm kick-off.

Tottenham Hotspur is the only non-league club to have won the FA Cup since the formation of the Football League and at the celebration dinner in 1901 members tied blue and white ribbons on the handles of the trophy, a custom which has since become a tradition.

Among several versions of the origin of Peterborough United's nickname 'The Posh' the one most widely accepted dates back to 1934. Supporters referred to the team as looking 'posh' when they kicked off in the Southern League against Gainsborough Trinity on 1 September, wearing a new strip. The word 'posh' was derived from people who took voyages to India for which the first-class passengers occupied port side cabins on the outward trip and starboard berths on the home voyage to obtain relief from the sun in the Indian Ocean. (Thus: Port Out, Starboard Home.)

Blackpool fielded Eamonn Collins, a Dublin boy aged 14 years 323 days, in an Anglo-Scottish Cup tie on 9 September 1980 against Kilmarnock. He played 15 minutes as substitute.

The first time John Hewie (Charlton Athletic) set foot in Scotland was to play for the national team against England at Hampden Park on 14 April 1956. He was born in South Africa and his father in Scotland. Hewie won 18 caps.

Middlesbrough claim to have had the first half-time scoreboard erected on a Football League ground in 1902. The first score it recorded was of Middlesbrough leading in an away match.

Before the 1914–18 war the season's first Football League matches were played in turn on every day of the

week except Sunday and Friday.
September 1 was the accepted
official opening day every year if it
fell on any day from Monday to
Thursday inclusive and, of course,
on a Saturday.

The word 'soccer' is said to have
arisen out of the habit prevalent at
Oxford University of adding 'er' to
certain words like togs (toggers),
swots or mugs (swotters or
muggers). Towards the end of the
19th century, the game was always
referred to as Association Football
to differentiate between it and
Rugby football, but it was at
Oxford that they took 'soc' out of
Association and then turned this
into 'soccer'. The word is often
attributed to one of Oxford
University's most famous
internationals , Charles Wreford
Brown. When asked one day

whether he was going to play
rugger he replied 'No – soccer'.

The phrase 'Ooop for T'Coop' was
coined at the 1885 FA Cup Final
when Blackburn Rovers supporters
came south for the occasion.

Blackburn Rovers full-back Bob
Crompton, who played 41 times for
England in his career, was said to
have been the first professional
footballer to drive to the ground in
his own car, an event which took
place in 1908.

At 3 am on 15 March 1958 the
respective managers of Darlington
and Lincoln City had to scale an
eight foot wall at Darlington's

Feethams Ground to obtain the boots of Ron Harbertson who was to make his debut for Lincoln v Liverpool after his transfer from Darlington. Liverpool won 1–0.

When Bebington referee Derek Owen learned that he was to be linesman for the 1981–82 UEFA Cup Final between Hamburg and Gothenburg, he was due to be linesman in the Eastham Junior League Under-14 Cup Final at Bromborough Pool.

The Swiss club Neuchatel Xamax derives its second name from Max, used both ways in the club's title, one of three famous Abbeglen Brothers.

Heart of Midlothian derived their name from the suggestion of the club's first captain, Tom Purdie, when they were formed in 1874. It was taken from the local nickname of the old prison demolished 50 years earlier but immortalised by a novel of the same name by Sir Walter Scott.

CHANGING HABITS

When Newport County were formed in 1912 the players changed in the King of Prussia Pub (later The King) and walked down Somerton Road to the pitch. Subsequently they changed in a hut in the corner of the field by Baxter's bakery.

St Mirren were formed in 1876 when the rugby team decided to switch codes. Their name is derived from the patron saint of Paisley, St Mirinus (St Mirren), who is supposed to have been a contemporary of St Columba.

When Arsenal won the Littlewoods Cup in 1987 it was not the first time the trophy had been presented. Made in the last century, it was originally called the Viscountess Furness Football Cup, contested by the workers at Furness, Withy and Co, north-east shipbuilders. The cup bears the mark of Turner Bradbury, a plate worker registered in 1889. Among previous winners were The Platers Helpers in 1923 and The Welders in 1966.

Underground electric heating wires were installed at Everton's pre-war practice ground in 1937, in an area behind the Stanley Park goal. During the war the area was used as a barrage balloon site. Army engineers ripped the heating system to shreds when they laid a concrete base. In the early 1970s an asphalt surface was put down to create the Everton car park.

Lancashire-born full-back Jack Slater signed for Bolton Wanderers in November 1906 as a professional at the age of 17. In the summer of 1914 he was transferred to South Liverpool. Before that this son of a publican had been apprenticed to a coal merchant. Later he became a millionaire from shipping and coal interests and was Conservative MP for Eastbourne for a time.

RELATIVELY SPEAKING

When Wolverhampton Wanderers were relegated at the end of 1981–82 it completed an unhappy sequence for the Clarke family. Wolves striker Wayne Clarke became the fifth brother to suffer a similar fate with different clubs. Allan Clarke was with Fulham when they went down in 1967–68, Frank with Carlisle in 1974–75, Derek with Oxford in 1975–76 and Kelvin with Walsall in 1978–79. Allan as manager of Leeds United in 1981–82 suffered a similar experience.

In May 1969 Alan Smith, 21, textile worker and amateur goalkeeper with Ossett Town was enjoying an evening out in the Showboat Hotel, Birstall when a stranger rushed up and told him in no uncertain terms that he should not be in such a place at that time of night. Next morning the stranger, Roy Lambert, Huddersfield Town coach, was left red-faced when full-back Alec Smith, 21, told him that it had been his twin brother he had been remonstrating with the previous night.

UEFA suspended the Stuttgart look-alike brothers Karl-Heinz and Bernd Forster after they had deceived a referee. The official was about to take the name of Karl-Heinz for a foul in the UEFA Cup game with Cologne. But Bernd hurried to take his place as Karl-

Heinz had already been cautioned and a further booking would have meant a sending-off. The ruse would probably have escaped detection if they had not told the story to reporters.

Swansea Town had four pairs of brothers on their books as professionals in the 1953–54 season: Cyril and George Beech, Bryn and Cliff Jones, Ivor and Len Allchurch and Colin and Alan Hole.

In the 1940s Millwall had twin brothers on their staff in Jack and George Fisher. Jack had a scar on the left side of his forehead since he had been a schoolboy. George collected one in exactly the same place in an FA Cup tie against Aston Villa. Both had a front upper tooth chipped in the same place.

Carl Swan made his debut for Doncaster Rovers against Bournemouth on 6 December 1980 and scored a goal. His father, Peter Swan, had played 272 games in the Football League before he managed his first goal.

During the 1959–60 season Leicester City had a former Scottish junior outside-left on their staff called Jack Lornie. At the same time

Preston North End had a half-back called Gavin Laing, who was also from Scottish junior. Lornie's grandfather and Laing's great-uncle had both played for Arbroath in the 36–0 win over Bon Accord in 1885.

Brechin City had twin brothers on their books in 1977, Dick and Ian Campbell. Dick, a full-back, combined his football with work as a planner in the Naval Dockyard at Rosyth while striker Ian was a P.E. teacher at Kirkcaldy High School. Both had had considerable Scottish League experience elsewhere, Dick with Dundee United, Cowdenbeath and Dunfermline Athletic; Ian with Dunfermline and Arbroath.

In May 1972 the father of the Leeds United and England defender Paul Madeley married Paul's mother-in-law. Thus his father was his father-in-law, his wife his step-sister and his mother-in-law his step-mother.

On 17 February 1973 in a Division One match, Newcastle United drew 1–1 with Wolverhampton Wanderers at Molineux. Kenny Hibbitt put Wolves ahead in the first half and his brother Terry equalised after the interval.

No two brothers in the game ever kept closer together throughout their careers than Scottish forwards Frank and Hugh O'Donnell. They were pre-war associates of St Agatha's School (Fifeshire), Wellesley Juniors, Denbeath Violet, Glasgow Celtic and Preston North End and during the war played with

Blackpool, Heart of Midlothian and Liverpool as guest players.

Alec Herd and his son David played inside-right and inside-left respectively for Stockport County against Hartlepool United on 5 May 1951 at Edgeley Park. David scored in a 2–0 win.

Harry Wait was Walsall's first choice goalkeeper in 1936 while his son Harry Wait jnr, kept goal for the reserves. In 1961 Harry Hough signed by Bradford Park Avenue from Barnsley was the reserve goalkeeper while his son Haydn was in goal for the 'A' team.

On 31 August 1953 Barrow fielded brothers Jack Keen (left-half), Alan Keen (inside-left) and Herbert Keen (outside-left) against Port Vale in a Division Three (Northern Section) match.

The parents of a boy named Steele took a chance by giving him the forenames of Stoke City internationals Stanley Matthews and Freddie Steele. He did become a professional footballer but for Stanley Frederick Steele, it was not at Stoke City but nearby Port Vale.

Fanatical football supporters have frequently bestowed upon their offspring the names of their favourite players, but footballers themselves have been less enthusiastic. However, after playing

and losing an FA Cup tie at Highbury on 26 January 1929 against Arsenal, two Mansfield Town players whose wives gave birth to sons, decided to name them Herbert Chapman Anthony and David Jack Staniforth after respectively the manager and forward of Arsenal.

In the 1946–47 season Joe Edelston was Reading's manager, daughter Kathleen was the club's secretary and her brother Maurice was a regular member of the first team forward line.

In 1969–70 Shamrock Rovers chairman was Joe Cunningham. His fellow directors included wife Mary, daughter Margaret, sons Arthur and Desmond plus son-in-law Fergus Campbell who doubled as the club doctor.

Fred Furniss made his debut for Sheffield United in the 1940–41 season against Everton at Goodison Park during an air raid. The all-clear did not sound until half-time. His nephew Ray McHale was signed by Chesterfield manager Jim McGuigan at the age of 19. Furniss had been transferred to Chesterfield in 1955. McGuigan joined the Bramall Lane coaching staff soon after McHale joined Sheffield United in August 1982.

Johnny Crossan, who played for Standard Liege, Sunderland, Manchester City and Middlesbrough and was capped for Northern Ireland, had three sons, one born in Lancashire, one in Sunderland, another in Belgium. Joe Cassidy, a Scottish International, had four children, born respectively in Scotland, England, Wales and Ireland.

Louis Page was one of four brothers who played baseball for England in the 1920s. He was also capped for England at soccer though his seven appearances in 1926–27 and 1927–28 were one less than he achieved at baseball. Between 1925 and 1933 he played eight times and was captain on five occasions.

George Berry was born in Rostrup at an RAF base in West Germany. He was brought up in Blackpool the son of a Jamaican father and a Welsh mother who came from Mountain Ash in Glamorgan. Berry's grandfather was Scottish. George's first international appearance was as substitute for Wales against West Germany on 17 October 1979.

Mr and Mrs William Keetley of Graham Street, Derby had 11 sons and one daughter. Nine of the boys played for Victoria Ironworks, though not Charlie, the youngest at five. Frank, Harold, Joe and Tom were the sons who played in the Football League. Four others, Bill, Albert, Arthur and John also played professionally while Lawrence and Sid were amateur footballers. Most of them were goalscoring forwards.

Tom, a centre-forward with

Bradford (Park Avenue), Doncaster Rovers, Notts County and Lincoln City scored 282 goals in 366 League games. He once scored six goals for Doncaster against Ashington on 16 February 1929. Frank also managed six in 21 minutes for Lincoln against Halifax Town on 16 January 1932. In February 1926 Joe, Tom and Harold played in the same Doncaster team and the following season Frank, Tom and Harold were with Rovers. Charlie scored 108 League goals for Leeds United.

In 1970–71 the Worthington brothers, Frank with Huddersfield Town, David with Grimsby Town and Bob with Notts County, did not miss a League game with their respective clubs. Their father was a former Halifax Town and Manchester United professional.

Fred Price and Clifford Price, his uncle, formed a left-wing partnership with Southampton in Division Two in the 1924–25 season. Billy Charlton (forward) and Jim Maidment (goalkeeper), his nephew, played in the same Newport County team in the 1920s.

The Milburn family of the north-east provided the rearguard for Leeds United at one time before the Second World War. Brothers Jim and Jack were at full-back while brother-in-law Jim Potts was in goal. Another Milburn brother, George, played with Leeds until his transfer to Chesterfield in 1937 while a fourth brother, Stan, made his debut for Chesterfield in 1946–47. Their cousin Jackie was a Newcastle United and England centre-forward in the wartime and post-war period while his nephews were the Charlton brothers Jack and Bobby.

Five Wallbanks brothers had professional careers with Football League clubs: James, John, Fred, Harold and Horace variously from 1929 to 1948.

BURIAL DETACHMENT...

In the 1945–46 season when the FA Cup was played on the two-legged system, Barnsley were drawn to play Newcastle at St James' Park and United won this first leg 4–2 before 60,384 spectators. The second leg was on the following Wednesday and lcocal collieries in the Barnsley area put up the following notice: 'In order that management may have knowledge of the numbers intending to be absent on Wednesday afternoon, will those whose relatives are to be buried on that day please apply by Tuesday for permission to attend.' There were 27,000 'funerals' and Barnsley honoured their 'dead' by winning 3–0, even though they missed a penalty.

ON THE RAILS

When did Manchester City become Tottenham Hotspur? The answer was in May 1937 when a B17 class locomotive of the LNER was renamed. But the following month another engine named Manchester City came into service. The full list of locomotives with Football League club names was:

2848 Arsenal
2849 Sheffield United
2850 Grimsby Town
2851 Derby County
2852 Darlington
2853 Huddersfield Town
2854 Sunderland
2855 Middlesbrough
2856 Leeds United
2857 Doncaster Rovers
2858 Newcastle United (later The Essex Regiment)
2859 Norwich City (later East Anglian)

2860 Hull City
2861 Sheffield Wednesday
2862 Manchester United
2863 Everton
2864 Liverpool
2865 Leicester City
2866 Nottingham Forest
2867 Bradford
2868 Bradford City
2869 Barnsley
2870 Manchester City (later Tottenham Hotspur, then City of London)
2871 Manchester City
2872 West Ham United

The locomotives were built between March 1936 and July 1937 and scrapped between June 1958 and August 1960. Ironically the first to go to the breakers was 2867 Bradford and Bradford was the only club represented to lose its Football League status.

AT HOME AND ABROAD

Liverpool goalkeeper Bill McOwen was the odd man out in his team's first ever League game in 1893. The other ten were Scots, leaving him surprisingly the only Englishman in it.

Liverpool midfield player Craig Johnston was born in South Africa, brought up in Australia, had a Scottish grandfather and Irish grandmother, is a British citizen and was capped at Under-21 level by England. Moreover an American specialist saved his leg from amputation after he had suffered a rare bone disease as a boy. He was turned down when he wanted to play for Scotland because he had England honours and in 1987 was selected for the full England squad for the game v Yugoslavia.

Alberto Spencer who earned his reputation as a goalscorer with Penarol in the 1960s, was born in Ecuador of an English father. He married a Chilean girl while living in Argentina and was capped by Uruguay at international level.

In a year from 1952, Wrexham had goalkeepers born in four different countries: Bob Connor (English), Archie Ferguson (Scottish), Bill Hayes (Irish) and Earl Godding (Welsh).

Sir Stanley Rous made his name as a leading soccer administrator at home and abroad but he was previously one of the most experienced referees in the pre-war era, controlling 34 internationals throughout Europe between 1920 and 1934.

When England played Germany in the Olympic Stadium, Berlin in 1938 the Foreign Office ordered the Football Association to instruct the players to give the Nazi salute to avoid any incident which might lead to war. England won 6–3. But the following day in a match between touring Aston Villa and a Greater Germany selection which included several Austrians, the players refused and gave a two-fingered salute instead.

Eddie McIlvenny was born in Glasgow and spent two seasons with Wrexham before being given a free transfer. He emigrated to friends in the USA and played for Philadelphia Nationals. In 1950 he found himself captain of the United States World Cup team which beat England 1–0 in Belo Horizonte, Brazil and was later signed by Manchester United.

Unfortunately the Treasury would not allow the transfer because of the dollar exchange situation at the time. His American club agreed to waive the payment until conditions improved but in September they wanted him back.

Maurice Cox was the first professional footballer to appear in the University Match a year after scoring the fastest goal recorded at Wembley. In 1979 he scored after 20 seconds for Cambridge, beaten 3–1 by Oxford, and the following year was again on the losing side in a 2–0 defeat after he had signed professional forms for Torquay United.

On 1 October 1977 George Best created a record when he appeared for Fulham v Crystal Palace at Selhurst Park. He had then played in all four home countries in 10 days. His previous games had been for Northern Ireland v Iceland (Belfast) and for Fulham v Cardiff

VIVA ESPANA!

The 9 December 1931 was not exactly Spain's day. They were beaten 7–1 by England at Highbury and at the after-the-match banquet the orchestra only had the old Spanish National Anthem in their repertoire and not the tune of the recently installed regime. But one Spanish player solved the problem by whistling the new anthem and some considered it the best any Spaniard had played that day.

City (Wales) and v St Mirren (Scotland).

On 6 October 1928 Newcastle United fielded ten Scots in their team which defeated Leeds United 3–2. The eleventh member was Ted Wood the reserve centre-half who was a Welshman.

While Derek Spence was playing for Olympiakos in Greece during 1977–78 his Northern Ireland international career was interrupted. The Irish FA selected him for various squads but their telegrams were sent in error to AEK Athens.

Hyde goalkeeper Charlie Bunyan who conceded 26 goals to Preston North End in an FA Cup tie in 1887 was probably the first footballer to coach abroad. He was certainly the first British coach to go to Sweden.

In Festival of Britain matches played between 7 May and 19 May 1951, Football League clubs completed 75 games against continental opposition winning 47, drawing 17 and losing 11. In the same period they played 32 games against Irish clubs winning 26, drawing two and losing four, while against Scottish clubs they played 11, won nine, drew one and lost one.

In 1965–66 Preston North End had 16 Scottish born players on their staff, plus the Manager Jimmy Milne and reserve team trainer

Willie Cunningham. The club's No. 1 scout was appropriately named Jimmy Scott.

In October 1961 Stranraer made their first appearance out of Scotland when they met South Shields at Simonside Hall and lost 1–0. A return fixture was played in December and South Shields became the first English club to play at Stair Park. They won again 1–0.

Cameron Evans left Glasgow Rangers for Sheffield United in November 1968. Within two days, during which he played in one Central League game, he returned to Scotland because of homesickness and eventually joined Kilmarnock.

Manfred Braschler of St Gallen the Swiss Division One club was born in Austria of Swiss parents. In 1978 he was playing for Innsbruck and was given his first full international appearance for Austria against Portugal. But he had been a Swiss citizen since his birth and an appeal was lodged by the Swiss FA to FIFA. Austria admitted their error and Braschler later made his first appearance for Switzerland against Italy in 1982.

Noel Parkinson had played twice in European matches for Ipswich Town before he made his Football League debut on loan to Bristol Rovers in the 1979–80 season. He played twice against Skeid Oslo in the UEFA Cup as substitute.

Edwin Dutton was born in England in 1890 of English parents but was raised in Berlin where his father had a sports business. He developed as a footballer playing outside right for Prussen Berlin and was even given an international appearance for Germany against Hungary in Budapest on 4 April 1909 the match ending in a 3–3 draw.

When Scottish born Danny McLennan took up a coaching appointment in Saudi Arabia in 1982 he had previously been national coach of seven different countries: Philippines, Mauritius, Rhodesia, Iran, Bahrain, Iraq and Jordan.

On 9 October 1949 Peter Desmond played for the Republic of Ireland against Finland in a World Cup qualifying match which ended 1–1 in Helsinki. The following Saturday he played at Hetton-le-Hole for Middlesbrough Reserves against Eppleton Colliery Welfare.

A week after declining an invitation to play for the England Under-21's, Walsall striker David Kelly made his debut for the Republic of Ireland scoring a hat-trick in a 5–0 win over Israel on 10 November 1987. Four days later he was playing in a goalless FA Cup first round tie for his club at Southend United.

Jimmy Rooney, Dundee born, became Australia's most experienced international when he played 99 times for them, including the 1974 World Cup finals in West Germany. He was dropped before he could complete his century because national team manager Rudi Gutendorf, a German, thought it was wrong for a Scot to captain Australia.

In the 1956–57 season Arthur Willis (Swansea Town) was often the only non-Welshman playing for the club's first team, while Paddy Sowden (Accrington Stanley) had a similar experience as an Englishman among Scots.

Swansea Town defeated Real Madrid 3–0 during a close season tour of Spain and Portugal in 1927. They were only the second British club to win there after Nelson's success in 1923.

Although Partick Thistle have never appeared in the European Cup, their former Firhill Park ground was used for a home game by the Swedish club Djurgaarden against Hibernian in a second round tie on 28 November 1955. The severe weather in Scandinavia made it impossible to play the game in Sweden. Having won 3–1 at Easter Road, Edinburgh, Hibs also won the second leg 1–0.

In 60 years of international football there have been players apparently capped for the 'wrong' country. Under the managership of Mike England (Wales), they could be formed into this team: Poland (Wales), Israel (Holland), Italia (Brazil), Espana (Mexico), German (Spain), Holland (Malta), Turk (Israel), China (Brazil), Brazil (Scotland), Welsh (England),

Jordan (Scotland). Substitutes: Wales (Scotland), Salvador (Portugal), English (Scotland), Jordan (France), Welsh (Northern Ireland).

Ladislao Kubala was born in Hungary and was capped by them at international level. He later played for Czechoslovakia and Spain. In 1961 he was a member of Barcelona's beaten European Cup Final team against Benfica.

Stan Mortensen made his international debut for Wales against his own country, England, at Wembley in a wartime match on 25 September 1943. He was England's reserve but when Wales lost their left-half Ivor Powell with injury it was agreed that Mortensen should take his place.

When the Belgian goalkeeper Jean Trappeniers came on as a second-half substitute for his country against Holland on 30 September 1964, he joined ten of his Anderlecht club members already playing. Belgium won 1–0.

Torino supplied ten of the Italian team against Hungary on 11 May 1947. The odd man out was goalkeeper Lucidio Sentimenti IV of the other Turin club, Juventus. Italy won 3–2.

UNITED NATIONS XI...

Charlton Athletic were the first club to have players from a full team of foreign countries. At one time or another they had recruits born in Mexico, Jamaica, Singapore, India, New Zealand, South Africa, Nigeria, Italy, Denmark, Sweden and Holland.

Birmingham had four international goalkeepers on their playing staff simultaneously in 1929. Dan Tremelling and Harry Hibbs were full England internationals, Kenneth Tewkesbury an amateur international and Arthur Slater a junior international.

In September 1970 Steve Heighway made his debut for Liverpool in a Football League Cup replay against Mansfield Town and on the following day he also made his international bow with the Republic of Ireland against Poland in Dublin.

Barry Powell was selected to play for the Welsh Under-23 team in January 1974 but was declared ineligible because he had played for just ten minutes in England's youth team two years earlier.

Louis Bookman was capped by Ireland before and after the First World War. He played for Bradford City, West Bromwich Albion and Luton Town at outside-left and was the only Jew to be capped by any of the four home countries.

In February 1960 the final of the South American Army Championships resulted in Brazil beating Argentina 2–1 in Rio de Janeiro. Pele was sent off after exchanging blows with an Argentine opponent and the resulting brawl had to be quelled by several officers including a general. Argentina finished with only seven men.

Bob Thyne became one of Scotland's international selectors although his own career for his country had started in unusual circumstances. On convalescent leave after being blown up in the Normandy landings, he was pitchforked into Scotland's team against England at Wembley in October 1944, at wing-half and despite finishing on the losing side in a 6–2 defeat, retained his place. Bill Shankly had failed a late fitness test.

The Cypriot team Pezoporikos Larnaca wanted Felix Frixou, a 21 year old playing for New Villa, a Derby park team, to play for them in the UEFA Cup in 1982–83. But he refused, as appearing in Cyprus would have made him liable for national service.

Eamon O'Keefe played for England's non-league representative team while with Mossley and then for the Republic of Ireland against Wales in 1981 while with Everton. After a two year wrangle over his eligibility, he was cleared to play again for the Republic by FIFA, by which time he was with Wigan Athletic. He also scored four goals as an over-age player in an Under 21 tournament for the Republic in a 5–1 win over China in Toulon, France in the following June. He was 29 years old at the time.

In February 1987 an award by a Scottish brewing company to 'honour the performances of a Scottish born player' was won by Tottenham Hotspur's Scottish international defender Richard Gough. He was born in Sweden.

According to a report in the Bangkok Post in February 1987, the Russian leader Mikhail Gorbachev took a lively interest in English football and especially Wigan Athletic. He had apparently ordered the end of jamming of BBC broadcasts because he wanted to keep up to date on the football results.

Eric Jones, a winger, had played for Kidderminister Harriers, Wolverhampton Wanderers and Portsmouth before joining West Bromwich Albion in 1939. He played in the three matches of the 1939–40 season before war broke out and on the eve of hostilities being declared, scored a hat trick against Tottenham Hotspur when Albion lost 4–3 at home. He guested for a number of clubs during the war as well as occasionally assisting West Bromwich. In 1946 he was transferred to Brentford and finished his League career the following season with Crewe Alexandra. He subsequently took up coaching and claimed to have worked in 40 different countries by the 1960s including Finland, Switzerland, Egypt, Belgium, West Indies, Denmark, Turkey, Nigeria and the Belgian Congo.

Of the dual internationals among the home countries Bob Evans was the longest survivor and was still watching Chester in his late 70s during the 1960s. He was already capped ten times by Wales when it was found out that he was born in Chester. After that he made four appearances for England.

On 14 May 1955 in a schoolboy international at Goodison Park, Liverpool born Joe Baker scored both Scottish goals in a 2–2 draw while Aberdeen born Alex Dawson scored one of the England goals. Baker later made full appearances for England.

CLUB NICKNAMES

Most clubs have nicknames. Many of them have more than one. Some nicknames have gone out of fashion to be replaced by new ones. For example, Charlton Athletic are rarely referred to as the 'Haddicks' these days. In their formative years the players used a room over a nearby fish shop in East Street behind a public house called 'The Lads of the Village'. The fishmonger was a keen supporter of the club and frequently attended matches with a haddock nailed to a stick which he waved during play. This is probably the derivation of the club's nickname of the Haddicks.

Nicknames generally fall into five categories. 1. Principal occupations of the town or city. 2. Derived from the name of the club's ground. 3. Club colours. 4. Animals, birds and insects (some arising from the colours). 5. Derived from the club's name.

There are exceptions. For one, Sheffield Wednesday in their days at Olive Grove were known as 'The Blades', the nickname usually associated with Sheffield United. Wednesday became the Owls when

they moved to Owlerton in 1899. But the district is pronounced 'Olerton', so the nickname is contrived. Incidentally Sheffield United were originally 'The Cutlers'.

FOOTBALL LEAGUE

Aldershot
  Shots
Arsenal
  Gunners
Aston Villa
  The Villans
Barnsley
  The Tykes, Reds or *Colliers*
Birmingham City
  Blues
Blackburn Rovers
  Blue and Whites
Blackpool
  The Seasiders
Bolton Wanderers
  The Trotters
Bournemouth
  Cherries
Bradford City
  The Bantams
Brentford
  The Bees

Brighton & Hove Albion
  The Seagulls
Bristol City
  Robins
Bristol Rovers
  Pirates
Burnley
  Clarets
Bury
  Shakers
Cambridge United
  United
Cardiff City
  Bluebirds
Carlisle United
  Cumbrians or *The Blues*
Charlton Athletic
  Haddicks, Robins or *Valiants*
Chelsea
  The Blues
Chester City
  Blues
Chesterfield
  Blues or *Spireites*
Colchester United
  The U's
Coventry City
  Sky Blues
Crewe Alexandra
  Railwaymen
Crystal Palace
  The Eagles

Darlington
The Quakers

Derby County
The Rams

Doncaster Rovers
Rovers

Everton
The Toffees

Exeter City
The Grecians

Fulham
Cottagers

Gillingham
The Gills

Grimsby Town
The Mariners

Halifax Town
The Shaymen

Hartlepool United
The Pool

Hereford United
United

Huddersfield Town
The Terriers

Hull City
The Tigers

Ipswich Town
Blues or *Town*

Leeds United
United

Leicester City
Filberts or *Foxes*

Leyton Orient
The O's

Lincoln City
The Red Imps

Liverpool
Reds or *Pool*

Luton Town
The Hatters

Manchester City
The Blues

Manchester United
Red Devils

Mansfield Town
The Stags

Middlesbrough
The Boro

Millwall
The Lions

Newcastle United
Magpies

Newport County
The Ironsides

Northampton Town
The Cobblers

Norwich City
The Canaries

Nottingham Forest
Reds

Notts County
Magpies

Oldham Athletic
The Latics

Oxford United
The U's

Peterborough United
The Posh

Plymouth Argyle
The Pilgrims

Portsmouth
Pompey

Port Vale
Valiants

Preston North End
The Lillywhites or *North End*

Queen's Park Rangers
Rangers or *R's*

Reading
The Royals

Rochdale
The Dale

Rotherham United
The Merry Millers

Scarborough
The Boro

Scunthorpe United
The Iron

Sheffield United
The Blades

Sheffield Wednesday
The Owls

Shrewsbury Town
Town

Southampton
The Saints

Southend United
The Shrimpers

Stockport County
County or *Hatters*

Stoke City
The Potters

Sunderland
Rokerites

Swansea City
  The Swans
Swindon Town
  Robins
Torquay United
  The Gulls
Tottenham Hotspur
  Spurs
Transmere Rovers
  The Rovers
Walsall
  The Saddlers
Watford
  The Hornets
West Bromwich Albion
  Throstles, Baggies or *Albion*
West Ham United
  The Hammers
Wigan Athletic
  The Latics
Wimbledon
  The Dons
Wolverhampton Wanderers
  Wolves
Wrexham
  Robins
York City
  Minstermen

SCOTTISH LEAGUE

Aberdeen
  The Dons
Airdrieonians
  Diamonds or *Waysiders*
Albion Rovers
  The Wee Rovers
Alloa
  The Wasps
Arbroath
  Red Lichties
Ayr United
  The Honest Men
Berwick Rangers
  The Borderers
Brechin City
  City
Celtic
  The Bhoys
Clyde
  The Bully Wee
Clydebank
  The Bankies

Cowdenbeath
  Cowden
Dumbarton
  Sons
Dundee
  Dark Blues or *The Dee*
Dunfermline Athletic
  The Pars
East Fife
  The Fifers
East Stirlingshire
  The Shire
Falkirk
  The Bairns
Forfar Athletic
  Sky Blues
Hamilton Academical
  The Accies
Heart of Midlothian
  Jam Tarts
Hibernian
  Hi-Bees
Kilmarnock
  Killie
Meadowbank Thistle
  Wee Jags
Montrose
  Gable Endies
Morton
  Ton
Motherwell
  Well
Partick Thistle
  The Jags
Queen of the South
  Queens or *The Doonhamers*
Queen's Park
  Spiders
Raith Rovers
  Rovers
Rangers
  Gers or *Blues*
St Johnstone
  Saints
St Mirren
  The Buddies
Stenhousemuir
  The Warriors
Stirling Albion
  Albion
Stranraer
  Blues

WHAT A COINCIDENCE

Len Shackleton has 13 letters in his name. He played for England schoolboys at the age of 13, made his first adult international appearance on 13 April 1946 and was transferred from Bradford Park Avenue to Newcastle United for £13,000. On his debut for United they won 13-0 with Shackleton scoring six goals against Newport County in a Division Two match on 5 October 1946. But the sequence of 13 was almost ruined that day as Charlie Wayman had missed a penalty for Newcastle.

The Van de Kerkhof twins, Rene and Willy of PSV Eindhoven and Holland were both married, had children of the same age, lived in the same house which was divided in two. In a League match in 1976 Rene was carried off with a leg injury in the eighth minute of the first half, Willy with a similar injury in the eighth minute of the second half.

Villa Park at one time held goalscoring records in both soccer and rugby. Bob Iverson scored in nine and three fifths of a second from the kick-off against Charlton Athletic on 3 December 1938 and the Australian tourists scored in seven seconds playing against the Midland Counties XV on 17 September 1947.

In four successive home matches in the 1982-83 season Bury, Fourth Division leaders at the time, had a player stretchered off injured. They already had Mark Hilton recovering from a broken leg when Steve Kenworthy was carried off with a similar injury against Colchester on 30 October. Against Torquay United on 13 November Paul Cruickshank also sustained a broken leg and on 4 December Franny Firth went off against Aldershot. Firth was fit to play against Bristol City on 18 December but Paul Hilton suffered torn ligaments and also missed the remainder of the season.

Terry Venables was best man at the wedding of George and Marie

THE TEAM NOW STANDING...

In the 1959-60 season Tottenham Hotspur just managed a 2-2 draw away to Crewe Alexandra in a fourth round FA Cup tie. But in the replay they won 13-2. After the match the Crewe team left Euston station from Platform 13 and arrived at Crewe on Platform 2.

Graham in September 1967. The same afternoon they opposed each other respectively for Tottenham Hotspur and Arsenal in the North London derby. Graham was subsequently made godfather to Venables' daughter. In October 1987 Graham was already manager of Arsenal when Tottenham appointed Venables to the managership of the rival club.

◁

In December 1941 referee Arthur Ellis was given his first representative game appointment to take charge of an FA XI against the RAF at Elland Road, Leeds. His only other senior appointments had been a first preliminary round tie in the FA Cup in 1937–38 and a first qualifying round match the following season. The officer in charge of the service team was Squadron Leader Jimmy Jewell the referee who had awarded the controversial penalty kick in the 1938 Cup Final between Preston North End and Huddersfield Town. Jewell, also a former manager, later became a TV sports commentator, the first to cover soccer after the war. Ellis followed him on the small screen many years later as a member of the 'It's a Knock Out' team and was also one of the founder members of the Pools Panel.

In a Division Four match on 6 September 1966, Barry Dyson and Kevin Hector were on opposite sides respectively with Tranmere Rovers and Bradford (Park Avenue). Both were subsequently transferred, and again opposed each other, Dyson playing for Crystal Palace against Hector's new club Derby County in a Division Two game on 17 September.

In the 1930s Charlton Athletic signed two inside-forwards Bert Tann and Fred Ford. The club converted both players to centre-half and they became rivals for the position. In the 1960s they were rivals again as managers for neighbouring Bristol clubs, Tann for Rovers and Ford for City.

On the last day of the 1929–30 season the two Sheffield teams met the two Manchester sides. Sheffield Wednesday had already won the First Division championship, United were trying to avoid relegation. Both teams won 5–1; Wednesday beating Manchester City at Hillsborough and Sheffield United winning at Old Trafford against Manchester United to escape the drop on goal average over Burnley, who nonetheless beat Derby County 6–2.

At Southampton on 21 March 1987, the club's centenary society lottery draw for £5,000 was won by Guy Askham the club's financial director. On the same day at Sunderland Lawrie McMenemy, their £4,000 a week manager, won the club's £500 weekly revival draw. A week later at Leicester, the City team had scored 1, 2, 3 goals by half time against Manchester City when lottery ticket No. 123 won a prize of £1,000 for manager Bryan Hamilton.

Alan Coglan the Barrow goalkeeper broke his right leg twice in consecutive seasons 1958–59 and 1959–60 in away reserve games at Sunderland. In 1962 he broke the same leg again.

On 3 May 1986 Heart of Midlothian, unbeaten in 33 games, just needed to avoid defeat at Dundee to win their first Scottish championship title for 26 years. If not, Celtic had to win by three clear goals at St Mirren to overhaul them. At Dundee, Hearts crashed to late goals by substitute Albert Kidd in the 83rd and 87th minutes, his first senior goals in the season. Meanwhile Celtic won by five clear goals against St Mirren to win the Premier Division championship. A week later there was further grief for Hearts, beaten in the Scottish Cup Final by Aberdeen, when their captain became the first skipper ever sent off. His name: Walter Kidd.

On 24 March 1987 two South London First Division attendances broke the previous record for the lowest post-war crowd in the division. Wimbledon beat Coventry City 2–1 with a 4,370 crowd at Plough Lane and Charlton Athletic drew 0–0 with Oxford United before 4,205 spectators at Selhurst Park.

FRIENDS AND NEIGHBOURS...

A week before Jimmy Neighbour made his first team debut for Tottenham Hotspur against Stoke City in 1970–71, he had played in the No. 11 shirt for the reserves against Fulham whose No. 11 was Barry Friend.

When France adopted professionalism in the 1930s they allocated several places for foreign players. Several Englishmen were signed including Fred Phoenix an Aston Villa right-back. He was signed by Racing Club de Paris. His idol was Arsenal left-winger Cliff Bastin and in the annual friendly between the two teams at Highbury, Phoenix had the misfortune to break his leg while marking Bastin.

In 1942 Alf Ramsey and Harry Evans signed for Southampton as players on the same day. In 1955 they became managers of Ipswich Town and Aldershot respectively on 9 August.

When Allan Clarke made his debut for England in a full international against Czechoslovakia in a World Cup match in Mexico in June 1970, he scored the only goal of the match from a penalty kick. It was his wife's birthday, his wedding anniversary and the anniversary of his transfer from Fulham to Leicester City.

David Grant and Brian Strutt were in the same class at school, the same Sheffield and Yorkshire Boys teams, with two junior sides and then were Sheffield United ball boys together. They then both turned professional with Sheffield Wednesday in the early 1980s.

Peter Dobing was selected to play for two different teams who were playing each other on the same day.

He had been invited to sign amateur forms for both Blackburn Rovers and Manchester United and was chosen for an 'A' team match. Dobing declined both invitations. Later he turned professional with Blackburn and later played for Manchester City and Stoke City. He made is debut in 1956–57.

At the end of the 1978–79 Nottingham Forest had lost 389 League games while Notts County had drawn 389 times in the same competition.

Eric Westwood played for Manchester Boys against Southampton Boys in 1932–33 in the English Schools Shield Final, the matches being played at Maine Road and The Dell. His first two League games for Manchester City were against Tottenham Hotspur at Maine Road on 5 November 1938 in Division Two, then at The Dell, Southampton the following week.

Goalkeeper Harry Dowd injured his finger after 55 minutes playing for Manchester City against Bury in a Division Two match on 8 February 1964. Colin Bell had put Bury ahead after 25 minutes play. Dowd went into the forward line and equalised in the 83rd minute. Bell later joined Manchester City.

Kevin Bremner joined Colchester United from the Highland League club Keith after a week's trial in 1980 signing on his 23rd birthday. On his 25th birthday he joined Birmingham City on a month's loan in October 1982. After being recalled by Colchester he went on loan to Wrexham, scoring for them against Reading on 1 January 1983. Loaned to Plymouth Argyle he scored against Reading again on 1 February and then on a transfer to Millwall he completed a hat trick over Reading with another goal in Division Three at their expense on 30 April. In 1985 Reading signed him.

Norman Kirkham made his debut for Leicester City against Hull City on 29 August 1949 and suffered a broken nose. On 12 August 1950 on his debut for Southampton, he injured an eye.

On 28 April 1979 Peter Downsborough made his 650th League appearance in goal. Playing for Bradford City at home to Crewe Alexandra he kept a clean sheet in a 6–0 win. The same day Crewe reserves beat Bradford City reserves by the same score.

In 1977 Manchester United signed 6ft (1m 83cm) centre forward Tony Whelan, a Salford born local. In 1981 they signed a 6ft Dublin born defender also named Tony Whelan.

Billy Meredith scored his first goal at St James Park in 1894 and his 200th on the same ground on 12 October 1907.

When Brighton and Hove Albion beat Liverpool 2–1 at Anfield on 20

February 1983 in an FA Cup fifth round tie they were bottom of Division One while their opponents were top 37 points ahead of them. Brighton's caretaker manager Jimmy Melia was a former Liverpool midfield player and their winning goal was scored by another ex-Anfield player Jimmy Case. Liverpool's previous home defeat had occurred on 6 March 1982 in a Division One match when Brighton beat them 1–0.

Queen's Park Rangers became the first Football League club to install an artificial pitch and it was first used in the 1981–82 season. The Rangers manager, Terry Venables, had, in 1971, combined with Gordon Williams to produce a novel entitled *They used to play on grass.*

When much-travelled Hereford United manager Frank Lord was a Rochdale centre-forward he was the victim of an unusual coincidence. He broke his leg on the ground in August 1954 and it happened again on the identical spot exactly three years later.

Outside-left George Bowater scored one of the goals by which York City beat Burton Town away in the FA Cup first round in November 1934. Later, transferred to Burton he scored one of the goals by which they beat York away in the Cup's first round in November 1935.

Playing for Tottenham Hotspur against Burnley in a home match on

5 October 1974, Mike England and John Pratt both put through their own goal during the first half. After the interval both scored for their own side.

In August 1966, Colchester United half-back Bobby Blackwood broke his jaw in a collision with Queen's Park Rangers striker Les Allen in a Division Three match. In the return game in December, Blackwood broke his jaw again in a collision with Allen.

In 1937–38 Wolverhampton Wanderers had 40 players on their staff and not one of them was a married man.

On 21 December 1935 the train taking Mr B. Ames from the Midlands to referee a Division

Three (Southern Section) match between Exeter City and Bristol Rovers was held up through fog and one of the linesmen had to take over the whistle until the referee's belated arrival, 20 minutes after the kick-off. The man who acted as linesman during that period was Exeter City's reserve centre-forward Jimmy McCambridge, who was a former Bristol Rovers player.

Bobby Knox, a Barrow forward, scored the first Football League goal by a substitute against Wrexham on 21 August 1965. He was the first number 12 to save a penalty kick when, as an emergency goalkeeper, he did so against Doncaster Rovers on the following 27 December.

In 1888 West Bromwich Albion became the first team to win the FA Cup with an all-English XI. From

1907 to 1937 they did not have a Scot playing for them.

Tony Brown scored his first goal for West Bromwich Albion against Ipswich Town goalkeeper Roy Bailey. He hit his 213th against Manchester United whose goalkeeper was Roy's son Gary.

Howard Vaughton, who was at inside-left in Aston Villa's 1887 FA Cup Final team, became a director of the Birmingham firm which manufactured the second FA Cup trophy in 1896 after the original had been stolen.

On 31 October 1978 Lincoln City transferred goalkeeper Chris Turner back to Sheffield Wednesday, the club from which he had been on loan for 25 days. The same day they obtained the temporary transfer of Ian Turner a goalkeeper from Southampton.

James Commins became manager of Southport in February 1929, of Barrow in November 1930, of Southport again in March 1933 and of Barrow once more in June 1945.

Chris Ball, inside-right of Walsall, was twice sent off in corresponding matches against Crewe in March 1932 and March 1933 by referee Bert Mee (Mansfield). At Hull in a Third Division (Northern Section) game with Wrexham on Christmas Day 1936, Ambrose Brown, inside-right of Wrexham, was dismissed

after only 20 seconds by the same official.

On 22 October 1955 Jack Rowley scored his 200th Football League goal playing for Plymouth Argyle at Barnsley. Younger brother Arthur achieved his 200th on duty with Leicester City at Fulham in another Division Two match. Arthur was first to the milestone by 12 minutes.

Mick Martin (West Bromwich Albion) was sent off in an FA Cup semi-final against Ipswich Town in 1978–79 and Brian Kidd (Everton) was dismissed the following season at the same stage of the competition against West Ham United. In 1985–86 Kidd was Preston North End's assistant manager when Martin was taken on a month's trial.

On 7 September 1985 Ray Clemence played his 1,000th senior game. It was a League match for Tottenham Hotspur against Newcastle United. The only other player active at the time with as many appearances was his deputy Pat Jennings with 1,087 senior matches to his credit.

In 1934–35 Harry Adamson was Bradford City's leading scorer with ten goals in the Second Division. That season the club also ran teams in the Midland League, Yorkshire League, and Yorkshire mid-week League and Adamson was top scorer in all of them.

THE THREE DEGREES...

In 1920 Chelsea signed three players from Queen's Park: David Cameron, Ken McKenzie (both half backs) and John Bell (right winger) who were all studying medicine. All three duly took degrees as doctors.

In successive home matches in the 1985–86 season Torquay United's attendance was 1,282 against Northampton Town and 1,282 against Orient.

Norman Stanley Wesley Bleanch, a centre forward, played for four clubs that carried his own initials: Newcastle United, Southend United, West Ham United and Bradford. Then he carried on his career with Wisbech, King's Lynn, Cambridge United and Kettering.

On Easter Tuesday April 1947 Walsall won 8–0 at Northampton Town. It was a happy occasion for trainer Harry Wait, who had kept goal for Walsall when they were beaten 10–0 by Northampton in November 1927.

Cyril Williams and Roy Bentley went to the same school in Bristol and began their professional careers with Bristol City together. They met again in 1949 on opposite sides, Williams playing for West Bromwich Albion, Bentley for Chelsea.

PLAYER'S NICKNAMES

Individuals and teams have had memorable nicknames as well as clubs. The Sunderland side of the 1890s was known as *'The team of all the talents'*. There have been many others.

Team	Nickname	Year/Era
Scotland	*Wembley Wizards*	1928
Austria	*Wunderteam*	1930s
Hungary	*Magic Magyars*	1950s
Manchester United	*Busby Babes*	1950s

The Latins have had the best nicknames for either individuals or for certain members of a team. The five forwards of the River Plate (Argentina) team in the late 1930s and early 1940s was known as *'Maquina'* – the Machine. In 1949 AC Milan signed three Swedish internationals: Gunnar Gren, Gunnar Nordahl and Nils Leidholm. They became the *'Gre-No-Li'* trio. Zaragoza's five forwards in the 1960s were called

'*Los Cinco Magníficos*' – The Magnificent Five. Argentina's '*Angels with dirty faces*' were Humberto Maschio, Antonio Angelillo and Enrique Sivori inside-forward trio in 1957.

Alfredo Di Stefano (Spain)
  The White Arrow
Garrincha (Brazil)
  Little Bird
John Charles (Wales)
  Il Buon Gigante – The Gentle Giant
Nat Lofthouse (England)
  Lion of Vienna (for a memorable performance for England in Austria)
Mario Zagalo (Brazil)
  Formiguinha – Little Ant
Renzo De Vecchi (Italy)
  Il Figlio di Dio – Son of God
Pele (Brazil)
  Black Pearl
Tostao and Zico – both
  The White Pele
Eusebio (Portugal)
  Black Panther

Leonidas da Silva (Brazil)
  O Homen Borracha – Rubber Man
Domingos da Guia (Brazil)
  O Divino Mestre – The Divine Master
Matthias Sindelar (Austria)
  Der Papierene – One of Paper (for his slender build)
Gunnar Gren (Sweden)
  Il Professore – the Professor
Ernst Ocwirk (Austria)
  Clockwork
Franz Beckenbauer (West Germany)
  Kaiser Franz

Jim Towers and George Francis (Brentford) were known as the 'Terrible Twins' in the 1950s. Their goalscoring partnership was renewed at Queen's Park Rangers and later at Gillingham. When Alan Warboys and Bruce Bannister linked up in a similar pairing at Bristol Rovers in the 1970s they were respectively known as 'Smash and Grab'.

REPEAT PERFORMANCES

Exeter City were beaten 5–1 at Millwall on 14 February 1982 in a Division Three match. As a punishment the entire team returned two days later only to lose a Midweek League game 1–0 against Millwall Reserves.

The new West Stand at White Hart Lane was formally opened by Sir Stanley Rous on 6 February 1982. Tottenham Hotspur had as their Division One visitors that day Wolverhampton Wanderers, Spurs first opponents at the same ground 74 years earlier.

On 6 November 1954 Middlesbrough succeeded in preventing Blackburn Rovers' leading scorer Tommy Briggs from scoring against them in a Division One game at Ewood Park but they still managed to lose 9–0. On the same day their reserves beat South Shields 10–1 but the following week the club retained the entire team beaten at Blackburn and they defeated Fulham 4–2.

Colin Court made only one appearance for Reading in goal during the 1981–82 season at home to Swindon Town on 20 February 1982 when he had the misfortune to put through his own goal. But in the same match drawn 1–1,

Swindon's goalkeeper Jimmy Allen made the same error himself.

In the 1890s there were three occasions when England were engaged in two international fixtures on the same day. The dates were: 15 March 1890, 7 March 1891 and 5 March 1892. England met Ireland and Wales on each day and won all six games.

The year 1913 might have been unlucky for some but not for Sam Hardy. He kept goal for England against Scotland and Aston Villa against Sunderland in the FA Cup Final, finishing on the winning side both times over two weeks without conceding a goal.

In August 1974 Kevin Keegan was sent off twice in five days, first for Liverpool in a friendly against Kaiserslautern in West Germany and then against Leeds United in the Charity Shield at Wembley.

Bryan Robson (West Bromwich Albion) broke his left leg three times in 1976–77 during a period of six months. His first break came on 2 October against Tottenham Hotspur. After eight weeks out he returned to play for the reserves

but suffered a refracture against Stoke. He regained his place in the League side but shortly after being selected for the England Under-21 team he broke his leg for a third time, playing against Manchester City on 16 April 1977; his leg was in plaster for 14 weeks.

In 1963 two 15 year olds from Scotland joined Leeds United from Glasgow schoolboy football. They were Jimmy Lumsden (Kinning Park) and Eddie Gray (Holy Rood). Lumsden spent seven years at Elland Road, moved to Southend United and subsequently became Celtic's youth team coach. Gray was appointed player manager of the club in July 1982 and promptly appointed Lumsden as his assistant. Later the two linked up at Rochdale, Gray as manager, Lumsden as his No. 2.

John Sissons was 18 years 214 days old when he played for West Ham United against Preston North End in the 1964 FA Cup Final at Wembley. But it was already the fourth time he had appeared there. His first visit had been as a member of the England schoolboys against Wales, and the next two occasions had been for England youth teams against Ireland and the Rest of Europe.

On the morning of Good Friday 1928, Sheffield Wednesday were bottom of Division One with 25 points from 34 matches and with little prospect of escaping relegation as they were four points below Manchester United, their closest rivals. But they began the long haul up by beating Tottenham Hotspur 3–1 at White Hart Lane, captained by ex-Spurs player Jimmy Seed. Spurs were 10th with 35 points from 36 games before the match. Wednesday went on to win four and draw the other four of their remaining fixtures to avoid the drop while Middlesbrough and Tottenham were relegated. Even on the last day of the season nine teams were in danger.

Swindon Town defeated Newcastle United in the FA Cup in the 1928–29 season and Ipswich Town in the same competition in 1947–48. In both matches the opposing goalkeeper was the same Mick Burns.

After losing their first two home games in April 1958, Lincoln City were struggling at the foot of the Second Division. But they won their next five matches and needed to draw their remaining game to avoid relegation. They made it six in a row, beating Cardiff City 3–1.

Stoke City met Bury seven times in the 1954–55 season without being beaten once. They defeated them in the fifth meeting of an FA Cup third round tie, won a Division Two home match and drew one away.

Towards the end of the 1915–16 season there was such a pile up of fixtures in the Scottish League that Celtic played two League games in one day, 16 April 1916. They beat Raith Rovers 6–0 at Celtic Park and

NOW YOU SEE 'EM. NOW YOU DON'T...

When Pegasus played Bishop Auckland in the 1951 FA Amateur Cup Final at Wembley there was a crowd of 100,000, the first six figure attendance for this match in the history of the competition. In December 1960 a friendly between the same two clubs was arranged for the White City Stadium and there were 327 spectators present.

in the evening travelled to Fir Park where they defeated Motherwell 3-1.

George Best's several farewell performances for a variety of English clubs were not all auspicious occasions. In his last match for Manchester United they lost 3-0 to Queen's Park Rangers on New Year's Day 1974, his final game for Fulham saw them beaten 2-0 at Stoke City in November 1977, and in May 1983 after a handful of games for Bournemouth he bowed out in a goalless home draw with Wigan Athletic.

Playing for Rotherham United in a Division Three (Northern Section) match against Carlisle United on 13 September 1947, Wally Ardron scored four goals and against Hartlepool United on 13 September 1948 he scored another four.

CHANGE OF NAME

Clubs who have changed names since joining the Football League

Club	Previous name(s)	Until
Arsenal	Woolwich Arsenal	1913
Birmingham City	Birmingham	1946
	Small Heath	1905
AFC Bournemouth	Bournemouth & Boscombe Athletic	1971
Burton United	Burton Swifts	1901
Gateshead	South Shields	1930
Hartlepool United	Hartlepool	1977
	Hartlepools United	1968
Leicester City	Leicester Fosse	1919
Leyton Orient	Orient	1987
	Leyton Orient	1967
	Clapton Orient	1946
Manchester City	Ardwick	1894
Manchester United	Newton Heath	1902
Rotherham United	Rotherham County	1925
Sheffield Wednesday	The Wednesday	1929
Stoke City	Stoke	1925
Swansea City	Swansea Town	1970

Aldershot dropped 'Town' from their title around 1937.

Clubs who have changed names since joining the Scottish League

Club	Previous name(s)	Until
Ayr United	Ayr, Ayr Parkhouse	1910
Dundee United	Dundee Hibs	1923
East Stirlingshire	ES Clydebank for one season	1964–65
Hamilton Academical	Hamilton Academicals Football and Athletic Club	1965

Alloa dropped 'Athletic' from their title around 1980.

TIMELY APPEARANCES

On 27 November 1954 Dundee United centre-forward Johnny Coyle was unavailable for the match with Alloa. He was replaced by a trialist from the local Osborne club, Billy Boyle, who proceeded to score four goals in a 5–4 win for United. Alloa finished just that two points lower than Dundee United at the end of the season.

Harold McNaughton had the unusual distinction of appearing in a Merseyside derby for Liverpool against Everton, keeping a clean sheet as the unbeaten goalkeeper, yet never again playing for them in their League side. Signed from Edinburgh St Bernards in the previous August, he made his debut on 23 October 1920 because first choice Elisha Scott was on international duty for Ireland.

David Halliday scored four goals for Arsenal at Leicester in a League game on the Monday before the 1930 FA Cup Final but was left out of the side for the Wembley game. Halliday was deputising at centre-forward for the injured Jack Lambert and helped Arsenal 3–1 down at half-time, to draw 6–6 with Leicester City, the highest scoring draw in Football League history at the time. The fit-again Lambert scored one of the Arsenal's goals in the final in which Huddersfield Town were beaten 2–0.

In the early days of an FA inspired crack-down by referees on so-called professional fouls, Peter Fox the Stoke City goalkeeper was sent off for handling the ball outside his penalty area against Luton Town on 25 September 1982. Disillusioned, he thought of quitting the game but decided to carry on after many letters from well-wishers. The following month the FA decided that deliberate handball was no longer considered as serious foul play.

Micky Cook eventually overtook Peter Wright's record of League appearances for Colchester United in 1979–80 but only after a couple of mishaps. He wrenched a knee when he was about to overtake Wright's 452 senior games, suffered a back injury getting out of the bath and then twisted his back climbing out of his car before a League cup-tie against Gillingham when one match away from 500 senior games. He finally reached a club record of 422 League appearances in December 1979.

George Harrison scored more goals in the 19th season of his career than in any other. In 1928–29 he scored 16 League goals for Preston North End. He had originally joined Leicester Fosse from Gresley Rovers as an outside-left in 1910 and had a spell with Everton. After leaving Preston he played for Blackpool.

Steve Graham, a trialist from Tayport Amateurs, scored for Forfar Athletic reserves against Brechin City reserves in September 1980 and ten days later scored for Brechin against Forfar in a Scottish League, Division Two match.

Gordon Smith was playing for Brighton and Hove Albion reserves at Swindon Town in a Football Combination game on 30 November 1982 when it was arranged for him to re-join his former club, Rangers, in time to play in the Scottish League Cup Final on 4 December. Rangers lost 2–1 to Celtic and Smith went back to Brighton helping the club to reach the FA Cup Final against Manchester United.

After playing centre-forward in the Brentford team which beat Southend United 2–0 at Griffin Park on 29 September 1979 in a Division Three match, Lee Holmes put his tracksuit over his playing kit and climbed on the back of a friend's motorcycle at 4.45 pm. He was off to get married at a church in Barking on the other side of London with the ceremony due to start at 5.30 pm. The pair arrived at 5.25 pm but Holmes did not have time to remove all his footballing gear before putting on the bridegroom's suit.

Exeter City were losing their Division Three match at Reading 2–0 on 20 October 1979 with 25 minutes remaining. Manager Brian Godfrey signalled to trainer Alan Beer to make a substitution, indicating that City's No. 6 Dick Forbes should be replaced. Beer held up the number board and the club's leading scorer Keith Bowker started to walk towards the touchline. Godfrey realised that Beer had held the board upside down showing '9' and was just in time to prevent the wrong substitution. Ian Pearson then took over from Forbes and managed to score a goal but Exeter still lost 2–1.

EXCEPTIONAL ALL-ROUNDERS...

Charles Burgess Fry beat the existing World long jump record of 23 feet 6½ inches in 1893 . . . Alan Hansen, Liverpool and Scotland, was a juvenile volleyball and golf international for his native country . . . Gerry McElhinney, signed by Bolton Wanderers from Distillery in 1981–82, had been a double international at boxing and Gaelic football and subsequently joined the Northern Ireland soccer squad . . . Everton winger Jackie Coulter, who made 11 international appearances for Northern Ireland while with Belfast Celtic, Grimsby Town and Chelmsford City as well as Everton in the 1930s, had also been roller skating champion of Ireland . . . .

On Boxing Day 1932 Jimmy Oakes was left-back for Port Vale in a Division Two game against Charlton Athletic at The Valley. The match was abandoned because of bad light. Three weeks later Oakes was transferred from Port Vale to Charlton and when the match was replayed on 26 April 1933 he was Charlton's left-back in the 2–1 win over Port Vale.

Centre-forward Andy Graver, playing for Stoke City, had the experience of playing against one or other of his former clubs in four successive Saturdays in 1956: v Leicester City away (FA Cup) on 28 January; Lincoln City away (League) on 4 February; Leicester City home (League) on 11 February and Newcastle United away (FA Cup) on 18 February.

Eric Houghton made his first-class cricket debut for Warwickshire against India at Edgbaston in August 1946 as he began his 20th season as an Aston Villa professional.

Arthur Banner had a pre-World War Two trial with Doncaster Rovers in their Midland League side against Boston United. To his dismay he discovered the player he was marking was Fred Tunstall who had been Sheffield United's cup winner in the 1925 FA Cup Final against Cardiff City. But during the match Tunstall gave him sufficient words of encouragement to instil confidence and Banner's display earned him a professional contract. Tunstall himself had signed for

United one day and made his debut the next when transferred from Scunthorpe United for £1,000.

In 1946–47 the championship was decided by a 40-year-old player who was making his first appearance of the season in the last game between Stoke City and Sheffield United. The situation was that Liverpool had 57 points, Manchester United and Wolverhampton Wanderers 56 and Stoke City 55. Stoke had the better goal average and their game was a fortnight after the others had completed their fixtures. United won 2–1, Pickering scored the winner and Liverpool won the championship.

In 1971, when Arsenal completed a League and Cup double, the occupations of their 1950 FA Cup winning team were as follows:

George Swindin – garage owner
Laurie Scott – sales representative
Walley Barnes – BBC TV commentator
Alex Forbes – coaching in South Africa
Leslie Compton – wine company representative
Joe Mercer – Manchester City manager
Freddie Cox – Bournemouth newsagent
Jimmy Logie – newspaper seller, Piccadilly Circus
Peter Goring – master butcher
Reg Lewis – insurance broker
Denis Compton – cricket writer

In addition, Archie Macauley who had then just lost his place to Forbes was working near Piccadilly Circus as a traffic warden.

Aston Villa defender Gary Williams had played more than 200 League games for the club without scoring a single goal. But in a Milk Cup, Second Round Second Leg game against Exeter City he scored twice in an 8–1 win.

Mike Sangster, the British tennis star, was competing in a covered courts championship in London in 1960 when he learned that he had been selected to play for Torquay United 'A' team. He caught the night train to Devon and scored a hat-trick the following day in an 11–0 win.

In 1986–87 Hamilton Academical reserves often used coach Davy Wilson as a substitute. The former Rangers and Scottish international

left-winger was 48 years old at the time.

In 1987 Nottingham Forest manager Brian Clough gave Billy Stubbs, a 20-year-old player he had signed from Seaham Red Star, a £10 note for shaving off his moustache, which in Clough's opinion made him look 30.

FOOTBALL SONGS

Original football songs are comparatively rare. Two of the best known are Portsmouth's *Pompey Chimes* and Norwich City's *On The Ball, City.* Other clubs have become known for the adoption of traditional or popular tunes, notably: Birmingham City *Keep Right On To The End Of The Road*, West Ham United *Blowing Bubbles*, Newcastle United *Blaydon Races*, Coventry City *Eton Boating Song* and Liverpool *You'll Never Walk Alone*. *Blowing Bubbles* did manage to get itself into the charts at the time of West Ham's appearance in the 1975 FA Cup Final.

Another record which was given considerable air time but failed to make an impact on the charts was the *Manchester United Calypso* an up-market tribute in some ways, to the Busby Babes. It was revived in the wave of sympathy which swept over the country following the 1958 Munich Air Disaster.

The British hit single charts began in 1952 and acording to the *Guinness Book of British Hit Singles* the following is a list of the most successful football discs.

Team	Record	Highest place	Weeks in chart	First date
England	*Back Home*	1	16	18.4.70
England	*This Time (We'll Get It Right)/England Will Fly The Flag*	2	13	10.4.82
Chelsea	*Blue Is The Colour*	5	12	26.2.72
Scotland	*We Have A Dream*	5	9	1.5.82
Tottenham Hotspur	*Ossie's Dream (Spurs Are On Their Way to Wembley*	5	8	9.5.81
Leeds United	*Leeds United*	10	10	29.4.72
Manchester United	*We All Follow Man Utd*	10	5	18.5.85
Manchester United	*Glory, Glory Man Utd*	13	5	21.5.83
Everton	*Here We Go*	14	5	11.5.85
Liverpool	*We Can Do It*	15	4	28.5.77
Arsenal	*Good Old Arsenal*	16	7	8.5.71
Tottenham Hotspur	*Tottenham, Tottenham*	19	7	1.5.82
Scotland	*Easy, Easy*	20	4	22.6.74
West Ham United	*I'm Forever Blowing Bubbles*	31	2	10.5.75
England	*Back Home* (re-entry)	46	1	15.8.70
Liverpool	*Sitting On Top Of The World*	50	2	17.5.86
Manchester United	*Man Utd*	50	1	8.5.76
Liverpool	*Liverpool (We Never Gonna . . .)/Liverpool Anthem*	54	4	23.4.83
England	*We've Got The Whole World At Our Feet/ When We Are Far From Home*	66	2	19.4.86

HAZARDOUS JOURNEYS

A quarter of an hour before their match with Hamilton Academical on 25 October 1981, Clydebank had only six players reporting for duty. Because of a fault at Old Kilpatrick on the Glasgow to Clydebank railway line, several other players were delayed. Two arrived with five minutes to spare, another sprinted one mile from the station as the teams were ready to change but two others arrived fifteen minutes late and missed the game. Clydebank completed their side with a player who had gone along as a spectator and they recovered from being a goal down to win 2–1.

On 25 April 1981 Stockport County arrived at Bury for a Division Four match minus three snowbound players. They played the entire first half with nine men and when they succeeded in completing a full side after the break, managed to win 1–0.

Matt Busby's initial grounding in the game was with his local team in Orbiston. They had a certain reputation in the area and the village of 32 houses was known as 'Cannibal Island', where visiting teams were never in any danger provided they lost. Rare away winners had to sprint from the pitch at the final whistle and collect clothes and other personal belongings the following day.

When West Bromwich Albion visited Luton Town for an FA Cup first round tie on 30 January 1897, Tom Perry missed the train. A special was chartered consisting of an engine and one coach at a cost of £50. Perry and the club secretary Frank Heaven were the only passengers. Albion won 1–0.

West Bromwich Albion completed a Division One game on 29 September 1894 against Everton at Goodison Park with only 10 men. Centre forward Billy Richards failed to arrive at the station in time to catch the train and he was suspended until January 1895. After a subsequent letter of apology to the club, Richards' sentence was cut to a fine of one guinea (£1.05) and the money deducted from his wages. Albion had lost the game 4–1.

W. E. Clegg had been chosen to play for England against Wales at The Oval in 1879 but as a solicitor he was engaged in preparing evidence for the trial of Charlie Peace and he had to work late on the case. He was unable to leave Sheffield for London on the Friday night. Next morning his train was delayed by heavy snow and the match had been in progress for 20 minutes before Clegg appeared.

Derek Johnstone of Rangers, who scored twice on his 1970 debut against Cowdenbeath when still only 16 years old, lived in Dundee. In order to train at Ibrox he had to be up early, travelling as a commuter before 8 am. From then it was a tube journey from the

station to Rangers ground and the reverse journey took him back home by 3.30 pm. He could have avoided all this travelling but had gone into digs in Glasgow only to suffer from homesickness.

David Mercer, Hull City's inside-right, scored all his team's goals in a 6–1 win against Sheffield United on 4 January 1919. The Sheffield team arrived late and the start was delayed 30 minutes. They had no gear as their basket had not arrived at Sheffield station. Hull fixed them up as best they could but boots were an insoluble problem. Because of the fading light, only 40 minutes were played in the first half and 30 in the second.

Edinburgh referee George Smith arrived in Belgrade to control a

European Cup game between Red Star and Banik Ostrava (Czechoslovakia) in November 1981. On the morning of the match he contracted food poisoning and spent two and a half hours in a hospital bed on a glucose drip before being released to handle, rather shakily, the match which kicked off at 4.30 pm. Red Star won 3–0 and the tie 4–3 on aggregate but despite their disappointments, Banik officials wrote to Smith thanking him for his handling of the game. Unfortunately they sent the letter to Brian McGinlay who had been in charge of the Carl Zeiss Jena v Real Madrid game on the same day.

In 1946–47 goalkeepers Matt Middleton and George Swindin were involved in lengthy travelling. Middleton lived at Sunderland and played for Plymouth Argyle while Swindin resided in Bradford and was turning out for Arsenal.

When Manchester United were still known as Newton Heath they arrived at Stoke on 7 January 1893 without goalkeeper Warner who had missed his train. Three different players: Stewart, Fitzsimmons and Clements all had a turn in goal. United scored first but lost 7–1.

On 26 December 1896 Walsall arrived for a Division Two match at Barley Bank, Darwen with only eight men, including a committee

member whose registration was rushed through for the game. Four players had missed their connection. After winning the toss and with the aid of a strong wind and the clever disposition of their players, Walsall managed to work the offside trap holding Darwen at bay for the first 15 minutes. However, once they had broken through, the home side quickly scored four times, adding eight more goals after the interval.

On Christmas morning 1941 Bristol City set off to play at Southampton in a wartime regional match. They were dispersed in three cars. The last to leave contained two players and the team's kit. This arrived first but although the referee delayed the kick-off, there was no sign of the missing vehicles. Southampton offered five reserves plus their trainer who had not played for years and a side was assembled with the aid of a soldier, a schoolmaster and another spectator.

The match started an hour late and 20 minutes after the missing nine arrived. One car had had a puncture, the other came to its aid and they all lost their way afterwards. Roy Bentley, one of the latecomers, arrived at the ground to hear a fan shout 'well done, Bentley, that was a fine goal!'

At half-time the Bristol City team tried to sneak Ernie Brinton in to the game as he was not unlike one of the deputies playing. They rubbed mud over him but he was quickly spotted by an alert linesman and despatched back to the dressing-room. But Southampton won 5–2, although their trainer scored against his own club.

Even more misfortune befell Brighton & Hove Albion in the previous Christmas morning 1940. They arrived at Norwich with only five players and despite completing a team with Norwich reserves and a few soldiers from the crowd they were beaten 18–0, the highest margin in the history of the game involving two League clubs.

Raith Rovers can claim to be one of few clubs who have been shipwrecked. On 23 July, 1920 the 'Highland Loch' en route to the Canary Islands was grounded on a sandbank near Corruedo in North-west Spain, after a violent storm. All hands survived and were taken by lifeboat to Vigo. Their vessel was later refloated. Little the worse for the ordeal, Raith went on to win five games.

Notts County was sunk in an Icelandic Harbour in the late 1960s. It was one of a number of Grimsby trawlers. There were 10 in the 1930s and 14 three decades later, all named after clubs: Aldershot, Arsenal, Barnsley, Blackburn Rovers, Carlisle United, Crystal Palace, Everton, Huddersfield Town, Grimsby Town, Hull City, Nottingham Forest (abbreviated to Notts Forest – the cardinal sin!), Notts County and Real Madrid. Aldershot and Everton both featured prominently in the 1973 Icelandic fishing dispute.

On 13 November 1948 Millwall were playing in an away Division Three (Southern Section) match at Fellows Park against Walsall. They had taken a 1–0 lead when their goalkeeper Malcolm Finlayson was kicked in the face and had to go to

hospital to receive stitches in the wound. In his absence Jimmy Constantine went in goal. Finlayson, accompanied by a director, returned in the second half with Millwall 3–1 down. They found the gates closed and were unable to attract attention to gain admittance. Finlayson had to climb over a gate and, still dazed from injury, almost made for the wrong end. He resumed in goal, and within 12 minutes Millwall led 4–3 and eventually won 6–5 with Walsall hitting the bar in the dying seconds.

Aston Villa once chartered a special train just to take their captain, Archie Hunter, to Nottingham. He was an amateur and his employer would never let him leave early for matches. In fact, in his early days he had played under an assumed name to avoid trouble at work. Hunter was the first Villa player to receive the FA Cup in 1887 in which he had scored the winning goal.

Swansea Town protested to the Football League when the fixture list was compiled for the 1935–36 season compelling them to travel from Plymouth on Good Friday to Newcastle the following day to compete in two Division Two matches. The League paid for first-class sleeping berths for the club. Swansea won 2–1 against Plymouth Argyle but the next day they were beaten 2–0 by Newcastle. Between the two games they travelled about 400 miles.

Lincoln City became the first club in Football League history to lose its status automatically when at the end of 1986–87 they were relegated to the GM Vauxhall Conference. They had been the only League club to have experienced three previous spells outside the competition. Elected to Division Two in 1892 they failed to gain re-election in 1908, returned the following year but failed to gain re-admission in 1911. After one season outside they came back but were thrown out again in 1920. However their secretary at the time, J. H. Strawson, was one of the prime movers behind the formation of a new Division Three (Northern Section) of which Lincoln became founder members in 1921.

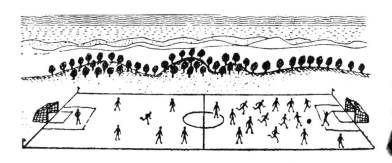

THE GREATEST HAUL

Paul Moulden scored 289 goals in League and Cup games for Bolton Lads Club in 1981–82. He achieved this total in 40 matches.

Opponents	Venue	Score	Moulden
All Saints	H	12–0	8
St Williams	H	16–0	11
Farnworth Boys	A	12–1	8
Christ Church	H	13–0	5
Sharples	H	28–0	16
Brenshaw	A	18–0	8
Moss Bank	A	15–0	6
Turton	A	14–0	8
Sutton	H	15–0	9
Marauders	H	14–1	9
St Peters	H	18–1	9
Marauders	H	5–1	4
Atherton RR	A	18–0	10
St Williams	A	14–2	8
Park Lane	H	11–0	8
Rose Lea	A	11–0	6
Farnworth Boys	H	14–1	8
St Judes	H	13–0	10
Atherton RR	A	1–0	1
Pegasus	H	6–2	3
Brenshaw	H	8–1	6
Marauders	H	13–0	7
Blackpool R	N	2–0	2
Atherton RR	H	25–0	15
Farnworth Boys	N	9–0	6
High Lawn	A	8–0	5
Rose Lea	A	9–2	4
Christ Church	A	7–0	6
Sharples	A	11–0	8
Sutton	A	9–0	6
Smithills	A	10–0	9
Turton	H	11–0	9
Smithills	H	13–0	7
Moss Bank	H	10–0	8
St Peters	A	7–0	6
Rose Lea	H	11–0	8
Moss Bank	N	11–0	5
All Saints	A	17–0	10
High Lawn	H	8–2	3
Marauders	A	14–0	4

Played 40
Won 40
Goals for 481
Goals against 14
Moulden 289.

EVENTFUL CUP TIES

Brentford were drawn away to Oldham Athletic in an FA Cup third round tie in 1926–27. Fog shrouded the ground and after 70 minutes with Oldham leading 2–1 the referee took the players off the field as conditions worsened. Fearing this might be only a temporary halt, Brentford manager Harry Curtis ordered his players into the bath. The Referee duly tried to call them back onto the field but abandoned the game when Curtis informed him of the danger to their health. Only then did the Brentford manager realise that in their haste, many of his team still had their socks and boots on. Brentford won the re-arranged game 4–2.

Hibernian were leading 2–0 in their Scottish League Cup tie at Dundee on 28 August 1950. The match had started with the spectators in shirt sleeves under a sunny sky but by half time torrential rain had waterlogged the pitch and the match was abandoned. It was not replayed because Hibs had already won their section.

Eric Tait, player-manager of Berwick Rangers, made his 500th appearance for the club on 7 March 1987. Since being signed from Coldstream in 1970 he had played in every position on the field including goalkeeper as well as scoring 114 goals. In February 1983 as team captain he became caretaker-manager and in the following month was appointed player-manager. On 12 August 1986 in a Skol Cup game away to Albion Rovers, he brought himself on as

substitute in the 58th minute, was booked a minute later and then sent off in the 60th, all without touching the ball.

Derby County were beaten 6–1 at home by Boston United in an FA Cup second round tie in December 1955. Boston had six former Derby players in the team including right-winger Reg Harrison who had won a cup-winners medal with County in 1946. Another ex-Derby player, Geoff Hazeldine, scored a hat-trick.

In 1980–81 Newport County in their first season in European football played 382 minutes in the Cup Winners Cup before conceding a goal.

After Grimsby Town had beaten Croydon Common 3–0 in a first round FA Cup tie in January 1911 the game was ordered to be replayed. Grimsby had left their opponents waiting on the field for ten minutes following half time while they had their boots restudded. Then 12 minutes before the end a linesman had to retire and hand over his flag to a Grimsby official. Grimsby won the replay 8–1.

Alloa Athletic began the 1953–54 season by losing 10–0 at home to Third Lanark in a Scottish League Cup game on 8 August 1953.

On 16 February 1980 John McAlle came on as a substitute for

Wolverhampton Wanderers against Watford in an FA Cup fifth round tie at Molineux and almost immediately broke his leg.

On 29 August the referee for the Brazilian Cup game between Atletico Mineiro and Flamengo in Goiana abandoned the match after only 35 minutes with no score. Four Atletico players were sent off and then the goalkeeper lay down on the pitch and refused to continue the match which was subsequently awarded to Flamengo.

Leicester City used three different goalkeepers during their sixth round FA Cup match against Shrewsbury Town on 6 March 1982. Goalkeeper Mark Wallington, playing in his 333rd consecutive game, was injured early on and had eight stitches in his right thigh. He conceded two goals, then limped off to be replaced by centre-forward Alan Young. But two goals in a minute enabled Leicester to level the scores by half-time. Two minutes after the interval, Young sustained a head injury and while he was off for ten minutes Steve Lynex temporarily took over in goal. Jim Melrose, who was substitute for the ninth successive time, scored twice and Leicester won 5–2. The match lasted 104 minutes with injury time included.

Raith Rovers were ordered to replay their Scottish Cup first round tie against 5th King's Rifle Volunteers in the 1894–95 season because they failed to provide goal nets. Having won this match 6–3, they were beaten 4–3 in the replay.

Scunthorpe United became the first Football League club to be eliminated from the FA Cup before the first round proper. In 1950–51 the FA had already completed their Cup plans. Colchester United, Scunthorpe United, Shrewsbury Town and Gillingham were elected to the League but only Gillingham, because of a cup run in 1949–50, were excused the qualifying rounds. Shrewsbury withdrew, Colchester played and won their tie leaving Scunthorpe defeated 1–0 at Hereford.

Chelsea won an FA Cup fourth round replay at home against Preston North End in January 1969 by 2–1 despite being a goal down after 90 minutes. They scored twice in the two minutes of injury time added on by the referee.

Three ties in the FA Cup first round were played simultaneously in the Essex town of Leyton on 22 November 1952: Leyton Orient v Bristol Rovers, Leyton v Hereford and Leytonstone v Watford.

In the 1925 Scottish Cup Final, Dundee led Celtic by a single goal with seven minutes remaining. Patsy Gallagher, known as the 'Mighty Atom', started a solo run for Celtic from the edge of his own penalty area, beating one opponent after another. Close to the Dundee goal he was brought down in a heavy tackle, but reacting quickly he somersaulted backwards with the ball held firmly between his feet and carried it into the net from which he had to be disentangled. But the goal counted and Celtic

then won the match with a Jimmy McGrory header two minutes from time.

When East Fife reached the Scottish Cup Final in 1938 with a shoe-string staff they were so badly hit by injuries that they had to sign two players expressly for the purpose of appearing in the tie. Danny McKerrall, a Falkirk reserve, was signed as East Fife had no other outside-left. Against Kilmarnock they drew 1–1. For the replay East Fife were forced to make another change, signing John Harvey from Hearts to replace injured left-half David Herd. But they won 4–2 after extra time with McKerrall, who scored twice, and Harvey thus winning medals in their first cup games for the club.

In the 1885–86 FA Cup competition, Burslem Port Vale, as they were then known, reached the fifth round without playing a match. In the third round they had a walkover when their opponents, Leek, were scratched from the competition. In the fourth they received a bye and in the fifth they scratched themselves after a drawn match with Brentwood.

The Scottish Cup tie between Inverness Thistle and Falkirk was postponed 29 times during the winter of 1978–79 because of a snow and ice covered ground.

The longest third round in the history of the FA Cup lasted 66 days during the 1962–63 season. It started on 5 January 1963 and was completed on 11 March. Ties were spread over 22 different playing days, there were 261 postponements and 16 of the 32 ties were called off ten or more times due to adverse weather conditions varying from frost, snow, ice, thawing rain and mud, to power cuts.

The worst affected was Birmingham City v Bury which stretched through 14 postponements, one abandonment and a replay, making 16 attempts before it was decided, while Lincoln City v Coventry City was postponed 15 times. Only three ties were played on the original date and the highest number of third round matches completed in one day was five on two consecutive days, 6 and 7 March.

When Crystal Palace won a cup-tie at Goodison Park in 1921–22 beating Everton 6–0, Palace goalkeeper Jack Alderson spent most of the game eating oranges. A contemporary report said: 'Everton were outplayed in every position except at outside-left, and that exception was due to the painful fact that Harrison never saw the ball.'

In the second round of the Football League War Cup in 1940–41, Barnsley were drawn at home to Grimsby Town in the first leg. The score was 1–1. In the second leg it was 2–2 after 90 minutes so extra time was played. The League ruling was that the match had to continue until someone scored. After a further 50 minutes the referee, Flying Officer McKenzie, was called away on urgent RAF duties and the match was stopped. The tie was awarded to Barnsley because they had finished in a higher league position in the North League than Grimsby in their section.

In 1930 King Carol of Rumania, a noted soccer enthusiast, threatened to shut down the British oil company employing most of Rumania's leading players unless they were given paid leave for the World Cup in Uruguay. The King then selected the squad himself and despatched them on their two month journey.

FOOTBALLING CRICKETERS

The gradual encroachment of the football season into that of cricket in the post-war period and increase of tours abroad by the flannelled fraternity has virtually ended the dual international sportsman in these fields. In pre-war days Middlesex cricketer Bill Edrich, a Tottenham Hotspur left-winger, quit the League for non-league football to concentrate on his Test career. But the last all-rounder at top level was Willie Watson who quit soccer in 1953 at the age of 33.

In 1950 he had been selected for England's World Cup squad. Wally Hammond, once a Bristol Rovers inside-right and Brian Close, formerly an Arsenal and Leeds United centre-forward, rank as the only two who have skippered England in Test match cricket and also become Football League professionals. Ian Botham joined them when he made his debut for Scunthorpe United in the 1979–80 season having captained England at cricket.

The following have represented England at both cricket and football:

Name	Football	Cricket
John Arnold (England)	Oxford City, Southampton, Fulham	Hampshire
Denis Compton (England)	Arsenal	Middlesex
Andy Ducat (England)	Arsenal, Aston Villa, Fulham	Surrey
Reg Foster (England)	Oxford University	Worcestershire
Charles Fry (England)	Corinthians	Sussex, Hampshire
Leslie Gay (England)	Old Brightonians	Cambridge University
William Gunn (England)	Notts County	Nottinghamshire
Harold Hardinge (England)	Sheffield United	Kent
Patsy Hendren (England)	Manchester City, Coventry City, Brentford	Middlesex
Hon. Alfred Lyttelton (England)	Old Etonians	Middlesex
Harry Makepeace (England)	Everton	Lancashire
Arthur Milton (England)	Arsenal	Gloucestershire
John Sharp (England)	Everton	Lancashire
Willie Watson (England)	Huddersfield Town, Sunderland	Yorkshire, Leicestershire

Chris Balderstone became the only man to play in first class cricket and soccer on the same day. He batted for Leicester against Derbyshire at Chesterfield on 15 September 1975 and an hour later, after a hectic car journey, he turned out for Doncaster Rovers in a Division Four match at home to Brentford.

On 14 April 1956 Mickey Stewart, who had been playing cricket for England in the West Indies, flew to Middlesbrough to appear in the Amateur Cup Final replay for Corinthian Casuals against Bishop Auckland. He arrived five minutes too late for the kick-off. Casuals were beaten 4–1. Their scorer was Gerry Citron who had been their marksman at Wembley in the original match and was to have dropped out for Stewart. Already capped for the England amateur XI

that season, Stewart turned professional with Charlton Athletic later that year.

Ten England cricketers of the post-war era have played professionally in the Football League either before or since: Wally Hammond, Denis Compton, Bill Edrich, Laurie Fishlock, Arthur Milton, Brian Close, Willie Watson, Ken Taylor, Chris Balderstone and Ian Botham.

Between 1906 and 1924 Andy Ducat maintained a career in both games with Aston Villa and Arsenal and Surrey for 18 years.

Viv Richards, the Somerset and West Indies Test Cricketer, played for Antigua in the qualifying tournament for the 1978 World Cup.

James Scot Symon played for Scotland against Hungary in 1938–39 and also appeared five times for Scotland at cricket between 1935 and 1938 including a game against Australia, the only player to turn out for his country at both sports.

Lincoln City had the distinction in 1982–83 of being captained by Phil Neale who was also the skipper of Worcestershire CCC.

Six members of FA Cup winning teams since the Second World War also played in first-class cricket: Raich Carter (Derby County 1946, Derbyshire); Leslie and Denis Compton (Arsenal 1950,

Middlesex); Jack Dyson (Manchester City 1956, Lancashire) and Jim Standen and Geoff Hurst (West Ham United 1964 with Worcestershire and Essex respectively).

DIED WITH HIS PADS ON...

Andy Ducat had a longer career simultaneously in the Football League and first-class cricket than any other player in history. As an Arsenal, Aston Villa and Fulham half-back and Surrey batsman he was an all-the-year-round non-stop performer from 1906 to 1924. He died at Lord's in 1942 while batting in a Home Guard representative match.

In 1966 Gloucestershire CCC had seven cricketers who were or had been Football League professionals: Arthur Milton, Barrie Meyer, Ronnie Nicholls, Dave Smith, Syd Russell, Harold Jarman and Bob Etheridge.

ALL IN THREES

On 18 December 1948 in a Division Two match between Lincoln City and West Ham United, City centre-forward Jock Dodds scored the first goal against Hammers goalkeeper Ernie Gregory who then had to go off the field with a fractured collar bone. Tom Moroney went in goal and Dodds scored his second against him. George Dick became the third West Ham goalkeeper in the match and Dodds completed his hat trick as Lincoln won 4–3.

Winger Ernie Shepherd played for three different clubs in the 1948–49 season: Fulham, West Bromwich Albion and Hull City and all three of them won promotion.

Dixie Dean once scored 18 goals in a day, in three games of six goals in each. In the morning he played in a Birkenhead Schoolboys trial, in the afternoon for Laird Street School and in the evening for Moreton Bible Class.

At the end of 1966–67 Stranraer retained only three players: full back Jim Shanks and centre halves Jackie McQueen and Jim Ferguson. Of these Ferguson asked to be released because he found difficulty in combining his football with a job in Airdrie. He was then given a free transfer himself.

In three successive seasons Millwall finished 14th in the Second Division with 39 points. Not only that but in 1928–29 they won 16 and drew seven games and scored 71 goals and repeated the figures in 1930–31.

Kevin Keegan's first three appearances for England in full international matches were all made against Wales: at Cardiff on 15 November 1972, Wembley on 24 January 1973 and Cardiff on 11 May 1974.

The Coventry City v Southend United match in January 1962 had been in progress for three minutes before it was noticed that both teams were playing in blue and white. Referee Arthur Holland stopped play and Coventry changed into red shirts on the field.

Harry Storer signed Martin McDonnell three times for three different clubs. He did so initially for Birmingham City in May 1947, Coventry City in October 1949 and Derby County in July 1955.

Chelsea defender Tony Dorigo who captained the England Under-21 team in the 1987–88 season held three different passports: Australian, Italian and British.

There have been two occasions when three brothers have appeared in a Wembley final, though neither were League games. In the Olympic Games final of 1948 Sweden fielded the Nordahl brothers, Knut, Bertil and Gunnar against Yugoslavia. In the FA Trophy Final in 1975 Matlock Town had the Fenoughty brothers Tom, Mick and Nick in their side against Scarborough. In each game the trio finished on the winning side. Sweden won 3–1 and Matlock 4–0.

On 26 November 1966 David Herd scored a goal against three different goalkeepers at Old Trafford when Manchester United beat Sunderland 5–0. Herd scored four times, the first three goals against three different goalkeepers – Jim Montgomery, Charlie Hurley and John Parke in that order.

Coventry City used three different goalkeepers in three sucessive matches in 1979 and not one of them conceded a goal. On 28 August Jim Blyth kept goal in the League Cup second round first leg match at Portman Road against Ipswich Town which Coventry won 1–0. On 1 September, during the warm up before the start of the Division One game with Norwich City at Coventry, Blyth injured his back during the kick-in and was unable to take part in the match. He was replaced just before the kick-off by Steve Murcott who on the same morning had played in goal for the club's youth team. It was Murcott's senior debut and he was able to keep his charge intact in a 2–0 win. For the return League Cup game with Ipswich on 4 September at Highfield Road, Coventry had Les Sealey on duty between the posts in a goalless draw.

Ronnie Williams played in Newcastle United's third team in a

League match on Wednesday 26 September 1934. Three days later he led the Wales international attack at Cardiff against England.

In 1924 Cardiff City succeeded in beating Arsenal on three successive Saturdays, twice in Division One and once in the FA Cup: 19 January (A) 2–1; 26 January (H) 4–0 and in the second round of the cup 2 February (H) 1–0.

Christmas Day 1919 was a double celebration for Coventry City despite the fact that they were beaten 3–2 by Stoke. The reason for joy was that the two goals scored were the first the side had been able to achieve in Division Two for nearly three months.

Jim Hall and Peter Price both scored hat-tricks for Peterborough United against Oldham Athletic on 26 November 1969. Peterborough won 8–1 and Hall actually scored four times. The next occasion two players each scored a hat-trick for the same team in a Football League match was on 9 October 1971 when Peterborough beat Barrow 7–0 with a trio each for Hall and Price.

The Cameroon had three different coaches in four months before the 1982 World Cup finals in which they were competing for the first time. They drew all three games including 1–1 against Italy the eventual winners but were still eliminated.

Orient defender John Sitton was sent off at Burnley on 14 December 1985 after two minutes. It was his first tackle and he had not previously touched the ball. It was also his third dismissal in three months.

Former Skelmersdale full back Tommy Roberts played with three different teams in three different divisions in successive games in the 1950s, first with Blackburn Rovers (Division Two), then Watford (Division Three, Southern Section) and then Chester (Division Three, Northern Section).

Former Football League referee George Reader became chairman of Southampton after retiring from the official list. But three other referees became Football League club managers: Herbert Bamlett (Manchester United), Albert Prince-Cox (Bristol Rovers) and Jimmy Jewell (Norwich City).

In the space of seven days in November 1946, Charlie McClelland played with three different clubs: Blackburn Rovers, Droylsden and Hyde United.

Manchester City were awarded three penalties against Newcastle United on 27 January 1912. Eli Fletcher missed twice, but declined a third effort. Irvine Thornley accepted the responsibility and although his spot kick was saved, George Wynn scored from the rebound and City managed to draw 1–1.

Goalkeeper Chic Brodie appeared in three different divisions in consecutive matches in 1961. He made his last appearance for Aldershot in Division Four on 4 February 1961 before being transferred to Wolverhampton Wanderers. He made one First Division appearance for them before moving to Northampton Town for whom he turned out in Division Three on 30 September. He later had a trio of misfortunes, being hit by a dog running into him at Colchester while playing for Brentford and having to quit League football as a result of his injury; having 11 goals knocked past him in an FA Cup tie for Margate against Bournemouth in 1971 and while combining football with taxi-driving having a road accident at Westminster, the driver of the other vehicle being Geoff Hurst, West Ham and England forward.

Roy Clarke made consecutive appearances in three different divisions in 1947 at outside-left. He made his last appearance for Cardiff City in the Third Division (Southern Section) before his transfer to Manchester City (Second Division) prior to the last game of the season. City won promotion to the First Division and Clarke's next game the following season was in it.

Ray Bowden scored a hat trick on his last Football League appearance for Newcastle United against Swansea Town on 2 September 1939, the day before war was declared. Ted Drake went one better scoring four goals in his last peacetime appearance for Arsenal against Sunderland.

'GHOUL TOWN'

This team, drawn from Football League players over the last 50 years, might figure in an imaginary 'Ghoul Town':

Steve Death	West Ham United, Reading
John Blood	Exeter City
Arthur Lawless	Plymouth Argyle, Oldham Athletic, Aldershot, Southport
Tommy Gore	Wigan Athletic, Bury, Port Vale
Bob Savage	Wrexham, Stoke City, Bournemouth, Bradford City
Micky Hazard	Tottenham Hotspur, Chelsea
Keith Fear	Bristol City, Plymouth Argyle, Chester
Abe Blight	Barnsley
Geoff Coffin	Chester
Mark Graves	Plymouth Argyle
John Skull	Swindon Town

A SWITCH IN TIME

On 26 December 1981 Oldham Athletic were beaten 3–0 at home by Blackburn Rovers. The match had been switched from Blackburn by mutual agreement because Oldham's Boundary Park pitch was playable unlike Ewood Park, Blackburn. The Football League at first ruled that the match would still count as a home fixture for Blackburn but altered their decision to record it as a home game for Oldham. It was Oldham's first home defeat that season.

On 21 February 1948 in a Division One match between Sunderland and Huddersfield Town at Roker Park, goalkeeper Bob Hesford fractured his right ankle in the first attack when he collided with Sunderland's Frank Bee. The kick-off had been due at 3.15 pm but the game had actually started at 3.10. By the original kick-off time Hesford was already back in the dressing room injured.

In April 1986, Everton signed Pat Jennings on non-contract forms as cover for reserve goalkeeper Bobby Mimms just before the FA Cup semi-final. First choice Neville Southall was injured and out for the season. Fred Barber was cup-tied. Jennings had only played one senior game for Tottenham Hotspur that season in the Super Cup against Liverpool in January. He was registered for Spurs in League games but his registration had to be cancelled before he could sign for Everton.

On 17 January 1987 Glasgow Rangers played just one game but won two matches. Their Premier Division fixture at Dundee was postponed because of bad weather, so they re-arranged a home game with Hamilton Academical and duly won it 2–0 at Ibrox. But the Pools Panel gave Rangers an 'away win' at Dundee as well.

Barry Dunn was 27 years old when he joined Sunderland from minor soccer in the Wearside League in September 1979. But George Shenton was a pre-war recruit for Port Vale from non-league circles at the age of 36.

On 30 September 1978, Bristol Rovers defender Peter Aitken was booked in a Division Two match at Cambridge United after 92 minutes and then scored a dramatic equaliser 60 seconds later. Three minutes injury time had been added on.

Tony Symonds, a half back, was given a free transfer by Bradford Park Avenue in 1967 after they had to seek re-election to the Fourth Division. He was promptly signed by Fulham, then in the First Division.

Glyn Jones an 18-year-old goalkeeper, conceded nine goals at Tottenham when playing in his third first team game on 22 October 1977 in a Division Two match for Bristol Rovers. Nine days later he was back at White Hart Lane in action against Spurs Reserves in a 1–1 draw.

Clapton Orient played two League matches at Wembley Stadium in 1930. Their ground was having an extension and no suitable alternative venue could be found in the vicinity. On 22 November they played Brentford before a crowd of 10,300 in this Division Three (Southern Section) match and won 2–0. They returned on 6 December to beat Southend United 3–1. Two days earlier they had met Luton Town in a replayed FA Cup tie at Highbury. Unfortunately their second Wembley visit attracted only 2,500 and the receipts of £100 were insufficient to guarantee Wembley's fee for hire.

After making his first appearance at centre-forward for Scotland in 1934 Dave McCulloch sent his shirt to his old schoolmaster at Hamilton where the boys were given a holiday to mark the occasion.

In the 1932–33 season Blackpool were sliding towards relegation when they decided to try Phil Watson at centre forward. He scored three goals in a ten minute

spell against Aston Villa but never scored again at centre-forward and Blackpool went down.

On 22 December 1979 the attendance for the visit of Stenhousemuir to Meadowbank Thistle was given as 80. Across the city of Edinburgh at Easter Road, Hibernian, with the attraction of George Best in their side, were entertaining Rangers before 18,740. When Meadowbank were drawn against Hibs in the third round of the Scottish cup on 26 January 1980 the tie was switched to Hearts ground at Tynecastle on police advice. Hibs won 1–0 before a crowd of 8,415.

When Chesterfield visited Darlington for a Division Three (Northern Section) match on 29 December 1923, the frozen ground was unfit for play. But the game was completed on the adjoining cricket pitch. Referee Bert Fogg obtained both clubs' signed agreement before the match, stating that they had been parties to the switch and would stand by the result.

Towards the end of the 1933–34 season Manchester United were in danger of being relegated to Division Three (Northern Section). In an attempt to change their fortunes they changed their colours to a design of cherry hoops on white. On 5 May 1934 the last match was at Millwall who were second from bottom with one point more than United. United won 2–0 and Millwall went down. The old colours re-appeared at the beginning of the following season.

Ferranti Thistle, founded in 1943, gained admission to the Scottish League Division Two in 1974 and were promptly informed that since their name had commercial connections they would have to change it before they could be allowed to compete. They then became Meadowbank Thistle and since their ground was unsuitable for League football they switched to the Meadowbank Stadium, opened for the 1970 Commonwealth Games. The 16,000 capacity enclosure is not open completely for football as only the 7,500 seats at the main stand are used for matches.

In June 1982 Wolverhampton Wanderers cancelled the registration of Peter Knowles, 36, who had left the club in 1969 to become a Jehovah's Witness.

In 1938 Hibernian decided to copy the Arsenal style of shirt though not their colours. They added white sleeves to their green shirts and discarded their black stockings in favour of green with white tops.

Goals in four seconds were claimed by Jim Fryatt for Bradford (Park Avenue) from the kick-off against Tranmere Rovers on 25 April 1965 in a Division Four match and by Albert Quixall from the start of the second half for Manchester United in a friendly against Bayern Munich on 8 August 1959. Quixall's effort was from a 58 yard shot and is slightly more credible than the Fryatt example.

Fryatt kicked off, tapping the ball to his nearest colleague and immediately made straight for the edge of the Tranmere penalty area 37 yards away, arriving in time to receive it after four of his colleagues had been involved in the passing movement. When he retired, Fryatt worked as a croupier in a Las Vegas casino.

Arthur Turner was originally an upholsterer but he was thrown out of work when the factory was destroyed by fire. Unable to find suitable alternative employment he decided to take up professional football and signed for Stoke City in 1931. He later played for Birmingham and Southport before becoming a manager with Crewe Alexandra, Birmingham and Oxford United.

To celebrate promotion in 1933, Tottenham Hotspur engaged the band of the Grenadier Guards to play at their first home match of the new season against Wolverhampton Wanderers on Monday 28 August. Unfortunately the servicemen were unavailable for an evening performance, so Spurs changed the kick-off time to the afternoon. Both band and team played well, Spurs winning 4–0, but many fans were unable to attend.

HONOURS LIST

Tom Whittaker became the first professional footballer to be given a decoration in the Royal Honours List when as Arsenal manager he was awarded the MBE in 1947. He was a former Arsenal left-back and trainer. Since then there have been numerous awards.

Knighthoods

Stanley Matthews	1965
Alf Ramsey	1967
Matt Busby	1968
Walter Winterbottom	1978

MBE

Jimmy Dickinson	1965
Ivor Allchurch	1966
Harold Shepherdson	1969
Walter Winterbottom	1972
Ian Callaghan	1975
Alan Mullery	1976
Arfon Griffiths	1976
Pat Jennings	1976
Terry Paine	1977
Tommy Smith	1977
Martin Peters	1978
John Trollope	1978
Geoff Hurst	1979
Kevin Keelan	1980
Trevor Brooking	1981
Billy Bingham	1981
John Toshack	1982
Martin O'Neill	1982
Eddie Gray	1983
Mick Mills	1984
Kenny Dalglish	1985
Sammy McIlroy	1986
Steve Perryman	1986

Peter Shilton	1986
Ray Clemence	1987
Billy Bonds	1988

OBE

Tommy Walker	1960
Tom Finney	1961
Bobby Moore	1967
Bobby Charlton	1969
Don Revie	1970
Gordon Banks	1970
George Eastham	1973
Jack Charlton	1974
Bill Shankly	1974
Bill Nicholson	1975
Cliff Lloyd	1975
Joe Mercer	1976
Bob Paisley	1977
Emlyn Hughes	1980
Bertie Mee	1984
Alex Ferguson	1985
Pat Jennings	1987

CBE

Stanley Matthews	1957
Matt Busby	1958
Billy Wright	1959
Jock Stein	1970
Denis Compton	1972
Frank McLintock	1972
Bobby Charlton	1974
Ron Greenwood	1981
Kevin Keegan	1982
John Hollins	1982

Brian Close was awarded the CBE for his cricketing prowess in 1975 but had also been a professional footballer.

PAYING THE PENALTY

On 9 December 1922 Willie McStay took three penalties for Celtic against Falkirk in a Division One match, missing two but scoring from a third in a 1–1 draw. Falkirk's goal also came from a spot kick.

During the Division One match between Nottingham Forest and Bolton Wanderers on Boxing Day 1934, Forest were awarded a penalty. At the time Harry Martin their regular penalty taker was in the dressing room receiving attention from the trainer. Forest refused to take the kick until Martin was summoned from the treatment room and when he did appear he scored to enable Forest to draw 1–1. But at the end of the season Forest finished bottom and were relegated.

Willie Brewster playing for Chelsea 'A' at Dunstable in April 1955, faced five penalty kicks yet still finished on the winning side. Three penalties were awarded, two were ordered to be retaken. He saved four times. Chelsea won 4–3. Earlier in the season on the same ground Brewster had saved two spot kicks.

In March 1955, Albert Broadbent, 20, of Notts County was selected for the Football Association touring party to the West Indies. He had been fitted for his blazer and tropical suit but at the eleventh hour wrote to the FA turning down the invitation because he said that he had lost his form. The truth emerged somewhat later that he was afraid of flying, though he regretted missing out on what proved to be his only representative opportunity.

Eric Houghton played for Aston Villa in 724 games and scored 345 goals including 72 penalties and 30 free kicks. He scored 241 in League and Cup games alone and also played for England on seven occasions scoring five goals. In his last game for Villa he scored from the penalty spot with the last kick of the match. The game was a Central League fixture on Boxing Day 1946 against Huddersfield Town.

At the end of the 1938–39 season, Bill Dodgin, Clapton Orient captain, was given a free transfer by the club. Over 2,000 supporters signed a petition urging the club to keep him. But he left for Southampton.

On 7 May 1986 Barcelona failed to score in the European Cup Final against Steaua Bucharest and found it just as difficult in the penalty shoot out which followed this goalless draw. Rumanian goalkeeper Helmut Ducadam saved all four penalty kicks from the Barcelona players and Steaua won 2–0.

At Blackburn on 6 April 1891 thousands of spectators stayed away from the England v Scotland match as there was no Blackburn Rovers player in the side. England won 2–1 and the second goal was scored by Edgar Chadwick (Everton) a native of Blackburn.

On 11 April 1980 Cray Reserves scored three goals in 30 minutes against Herne Bay Reserves in the Kent League, Division Two. Herne Bay's normal penalty taker was replaced in the second half because he felt unwell, so when they were awarded a penalty, George Evans who had been fouled, took the kick and scored in the 56th minute. Four minutes later he added a second penalty and in the 61st minute made it three successful penalties to level the scores. Then Herne Bay went ahead 4–3. Cray then had a penalty themselves, but missed it.

In the 1980–81 season Dragan Pantelic, Yugoslavia's international goalkeeper playing for Radnicki Nis, scored a hat trick of penalty kicks in a Division One match against NK Zagreb and in the last minute saved a penalty himself. Radnicki won 4–0.

A stopwatch timing of the 1984 Skol Cup Final between Rangers and Dundee United revealed that there were only 56 minutes 39 seconds of actual play in the 90 minutes. There were 143 stoppages caused by 47 fouls, six corners, 20 goal-kicks, 64 throw-ins and six off-sides. Referee Brian McGinlay also allowed two minutes seven seconds overtime.

Everton goalkeeper George Burnett was transfer-listed and signed for South Liverpool. Twenty four hours later Everton goalkeeper Ted Sagar was injured and Burnett was re-signed by his former club as South Liverpool immediately agreed to release him. In October 1951 he was transferred to Oldham Athletic. In 1955 he collected his Provident fund money at 35 and joined Ellesmere Port. A year later Oldham wanted him back but as he had taken the money he could not return.

Carlisle United striker Frank Clarke missed a penalty against Orient on 4 December 1976 which had been conceded by his brother Derek Clarke.

When Dave McIntosh broke his arm playing for Sheffield Wednesday against Preston North End on 26 August 1953, Norman Curtis, the club's usual penalty taker, took over between the posts. Despite saving two penalties himself Wednesday still lost 6–0.

Frank Smith's career as a goalkeeper at Tottenham Hotspur up to 1962 consisted of eight years without a senior outing, never once being

OUT OF SIGHT...

Before the start of the 1957–58 season Johnny Morris was sent off in Leicester City's practice match because he told the referee he needed spectacles. He was suspended for a fortnight.

The first FA Cup meeting between Stoke City and Port Vale was held at Stoke on 15 October 1887. It was followed by a court action. Stoke won the match 1–0, but a few weeks later their goalkeeper William Rowley was sued by Vale for a breach of contract along with another player. Stoke had to publish an apology, pay £20 to a Burslem charity, the same amount to Vale for legal fees and release a player to their rivals.

On 8 December 1979 Clyde beat Airdrieonians 2–1 in a Scottish Division One match at Shawfield. Neil Hood scored both Clyde goals, conceded the penalty from which Airdrie obtained their goal and was sent off the field before the end of the match.

On 19 January 1980 Dixie McNeil was sent off as he was waiting to take a penalty kick for Wrexham against Charlton Athletic. With the scores level at 2–2 on the Racecourse Ground, Wrexham were awarded a penalty in the closing minutes and visiting players first protested and then indulged in some gamesmanship tactics while McNeil was waiting to take the kick. Eventually McNeil's patience evaporated and he kicked the ball into the crowd and was promptly sent off by the referee who had booked him earlier in the match. It was left to Mick Vinter to score from the spot and give Wrexham a 3–2 win.

On 22 March 1958 Walsall centre-forward Tony Richards missed a penalty kick in a League match at

12th man and never included on any overseas tours. He was then transferred to Queen's Park Rangers and made 64 League appearances.

When Peter Knowles headed a goal for Wolverhampton Wanderers at Portsmouth in February 1967, he was so delighted that he kicked the ball over the stand and out of the ground. It was not retrieved and Knowles later received a bill, which he paid, for £7. 10s (£7.50) from Portsmouth asking for the cost of a new one.

Bury striker John Murray scored a hat trick against Doncaster Rovers in March 1973 and was later sent off.

On 23 February 1957 Jim Iley missed two penalty kicks in four minutes for Sheffield United against Notts County in a Division Two match. His first shot was saved, the second hit a post. The incidents came in a 2–2 draw. On 13 October 1956 he had scored two penalties against Notts County in a 5–1 win at Bramall Lane.

Swindon. Later in the same game he took over in goal from the injured John Savage and saved a penalty.

In 1934–35 there were 394 penalty kicks awarded in 1,848 Football League matches, but 131 of them were missed.

In January 1955 Trinidad footballer Selwyn Baptiste was suspended for 1,000 years after playing in a cup game the day after he started a two-year suspension.

Fred Mearns, Kettering goalkeeper, saved 19 penalties in the Southern League during 1903–4. Later in his career he played for Sunderland, Tottenham Hotspur, Bradford City, Bury, Barnsley and Leicester City.

In December 1964 Aldershot goalkeeper Dave Jones was recovering from a broken leg and was given a run out in the reserves against Swindon Town. He saved two penalties while another was hit over the crossbar. Aldershot still lost 3–2.

Colchester United reckoned they had lost £700 worth of footballs in private gardens at the open end of their Layer Road ground in 1987. They erected a net to stop the disappearances but the residents objected.

BIRD NAMED

This team selected from post-war Football League players should really 'fly':

John Wren	Rotherham United
John Sparrow	Chelsea, Exeter City, Crystal Palace
Hugh Swift	Sheffield Wednesday
John Bird	Newport County, Swansea City
Barry Swallow	Doncaster Rovers, Crewe Alexandra, Barnsley, Bradford City, York City
Albert Nightingale	Sheffield United, Huddersfield Town, Blackburn Rovers, Leeds United
Roy Finch	West Bromwich Albion, Lincoln City
Ronnie Starling	Hull City, Newcastle United, Sheffield Wednesday, Aston Villa
Neil Martin	Sunderland, Coventry City, Nottingham Forest, Brighton & Hove Albion, Crystal Palace
Ian Robins	**Oldham Athletic, Bury, Huddersfield Town**
Peter Phoenix	Oldham Athletic, Rochdale, Exeter City, Southport, Stockport County

Substitutes: Alan Eagles (Orient, Colchester United, Aldershot), Brian Heron (Oxford United, Scunthorpe United).

FIRST THINGS FIRST

George Richardson was working as a miner in the pit at Manton Colliery on the morning of Saturday, 8 April 1933. In the afternoon he played in the Colliery team and immediately afterwards was transferred to Huddersfield Town, playing in their Central League side on the Monday and the first team two days later.

Alan Ball scored in the first minute in different Football League matches against the same team on the same ground. Playing for Arsenal against West Ham United at Highbury on 29 August 1972, he scored in 40 seconds and then again on 20 March 1976 after 55 seconds.

In 1985 Caernarfon left the North West Counties League and joined the Multipart League. But they had to wait 1,710 minutes for their first win in the competition. The following season they finished third in the league and also knocked out of the FA Cup two League clubs, Stockport County and York City.

Queen of the South's first foreign tour took place in May 1936. They played three games in France before moving on to Luxembourg and then North Africa. In Algiers they beat Spain's Racing Santander 1–0. Spectators pelted the Queen's players with stones; one player broke his collar bone, another was sent off only to return and for a time Queen's had 12 players on the pitch.

When Ian Stewart scored the only goal for Northern Ireland against West Germany on 17 November 1982 at Windsor Park, Belfast it was his first in senior soccer. At one time on the dole in his younger days he had played the guitar to earn a living.

York City were so determined to sign George Lee before other interested clubs could offer him terms that he became a professional with them in 1936 at the age of 17 years 30 seconds. York officials visited him on the midnight hour with signing on forms.

Bill Norman was appointed secretary manager of Hartlepools United during the 1926–27 season and remained in charge until 1931. One morning during his reign the players reported for training but were reluctant to change on a bitterly cold snowy day. Not expecting them to do anything he was unprepared for, Norman stripped off completely and proceeded to roll in the snow.

When Birmingham City goalkeeper Tony Coton, 19, made his debut his first touch of the ball was after 85 seconds and came when he saved a penalty against Sunderland on 27 December 1980. City won 3–2.

Of ten Division Two matches played on 18 October 1980 seven were drawn and the other three won by visiting teams, the first time in the history of the Football League that so many matches had been completed in one division without a home win.

Andrew Smailes, signed on a month's trial by Rotherham United in August 1929, remained with the club for 29 years. He became trainer in 1933, manager in 1952 and left in October 1958.

Tottenham Hotspur were not the first Football League club to have signed Argentine players. In October 1937 half back Augustus Corpa and inside left Casco Rinaldi were signed by Third Division (Northern Section) club Barrow.

Wilf Milne, the Swansea Town left-back, played in 500 League matches for the club before scoring his first goal. It was in the 1933–34 season and he went on to make 587 appearances. Steve Whitworth the Leicester City full-back who later played for Sunderland and Bolton Wanderers had not scored in over 500 League games before he became Mansfield Town's penalty taker in 1984–85, his last season in the competition. Yet in 1971 his goal

for Leicester against Liverpool had won the Charity Shield.

The first Football League matches were played on 8 September 1888 and the highest attendance of the inaugural day was 6,000 for Preston North End's 5–2 win over Burnley.

When Ipswich Town reached the 1978 FA Cup Final at Wembley it was not the first time they had played at the Empire Stadium. On 13 October 1928 before their entry into the Football League nearly ten years later, their Southern Amateur League fixture with Ealing Association was played at Wembley Stadium instead of at nearby Corfton Road where the pitch was declared unfit. Ipswich won 4–0 in front of a 1,200 crowd.

Keith Peacock was Charlton Athletic's substitute at Bolton on the opening day of the 1965–66 season, the first in which players were allowed to be replaced for injury only. In the early stages goalkeeper Mike Rose was injured, John Hewie took over in goal and Peacock came on in the No. 12 shirt. It was only on the way home that evening that Peacock read that he had been the first substitute to appear in a Football League game, though the newspaper referred to him as Keith Piggot!

Billy Whitehurst played for Retford Town, Bridlington Trinity and Mexborough while working as a bricklayer. While with Mexborough in 1980–81 he was selected to play for a Midland League Select XI against Nottingham Forest Reserves. A scout from Hull City was present and afterwards invited Whitehurst, 19, to play for Hull Reserves against Notts County on the following Tuesday. Two days later he signed and made his senior debut against Gillingham on the Saturday. But Hull lost 2–0.

Bobby Thomson signed as an amateur for Albion Rovers at 16, made his debut for Airdrieonians at the same age and joined Wolverhampton Wanderers when he was 17.

The fastest goal scored by a player making his debut was credited to Bernard Evans playing for

A FOUR-LEGGED FRIENDLY

When Stirling Albion arranged a friendly match with the Austrian club Admira on 17 April 1954 the club's chairman, Tom Fergusson, invited Hollywood star Roy Rogers, his wife Dale Evans and horse Trigger to give a half time display.

Wrexham at Bradford in September 1954 when he scored after 25 seconds.

Malcolm Clarke was the first substitute making his debut in the Football League not to make

contact with the ball. He came on for Leicester City against Leeds United on 25 September 1965, 90 seconds from time.

Mansfield Town's first Division Three home goal of the 1971–72 season, scored by John Fairbrother against Plymouth Argyle on 18 December, was not registered until they had played for seven minutes short of 14 hours on their Field Mill ground in the Football League during the season. It was their tenth home League game. Yet they had previously scored six times in two FA Cup ties at home, 4–3 v Chester and 2–2 v Tranmere Rovers.

James Forrest of Blackburn Rovers was the first professional to assist England against Scotland. It was on 21 March 1885 and Forrest had already played for England in their three previous international matches. Scotland protested about his inclusion and the England team manager made him wear a different jersey which was white but a closer fit than the others. His wages were £1 a week from Blackburn but he received £1 for playing for England so Rovers didn't pay him that week.

The first footballer to be specially flown to a match in this country was an amateur and the club involved was Bristol Rovers in the 1932–33 season. Injuries made it necessary for Manager Captain Prince-Cox to arrange for amateur centre-forward Vivian Gibbins to assist. Gibbins was a schoolmaster and was flown from Romford to Filton after school and arrived half an hour before the 6.15 pm kick-off. Rovers beat Southend United 3–1 on that 7 September 1932.

RIGHT ROYAL GOINGS ON

King George V first attended a match when he watched the 1914 FA Cup Final between Burnley and Liverpool at Crystal Palace. Burnley won 1–0 and their captain Tommy Boyle became the first man to receive the trophy from a reigning monarch.

In 1923 the Duke (later to become King George VI) and Duchess of York accompanied by the Earl and Countess of Strathmore attended Forfar Athletic's match with Albion Rovers. The Strathmore estate at Glamis was close by and the nobility were regular visitors to Station Park during this era.

On 18 September 1917 Ibrox Park, the home of Glasgow Rangers, was used to stage a Royal investiture, King George V travelling north to present medals and decorations.

Wembley Stadium has been a frequently used venue by the monarchy for cup finals and other important representative matches and in July 1955 the Duke of Edinburgh was elected President of the Football Association.

In February 1923 the Duke of York attended a second round Scottish Cup tie between Queen's Park and Bathgate at Hampden Park. The match ended in a 1–1 draw with Queen's Park winning the replay 1–0.

In February 1969 Her Majesty the Queen named one of her racehorses Charlton after Jack and Bobby Charlton.

This 'upper crust' team has been drawn from Football League players past and present:

George Duke	Luton Town, Bournemouth
Stan Earl	Portsmouth, Orient, Swindon Town
Bobby Noble	Bury, Barrow, Colchester United, Southport, Darlington
David Court	Arsenal, Luton Town, Brentford
Ian King	Leicester City, Charlton Athletic
Frankie Prince	Bristol Rovers, Exeter City
Peter Knight	Nottingham Forest, Oxford United, Reading
Kevin Baron	Liverpool, Southend United, Northampton Town, Aldershot
Frank Lord	Rochdale, Crewe Alexandra, Plymouth Argyle, Stockport County, Blackburn Rovers, Chesterfield
Gerry Queen	Crystal Palace, Orient
David Crown	Brentford, Portsmouth, Exeter City (on loan), Reading, Cambridge United, Southend United.

UNIQUE SITUATIONS

The League in the Scilly Isles is the world's smallest with just two teams in it. Both are sponsored by a double-glazing company and play each other every week. Imagine the excitement when the cup draw is about to be made!

Ian Rush joined Liverpool from Chester in May 1980 for £300,000 and proved an admirable scoring talisman for the Anfield club until he was transferred to Juventus at the end of the 1986–87 season. Whenever Rush scored a goal, Liverpool remained unbeaten. It happened on 144 occasions.

In an economy drive in April 1986, Rochdale manager Vic Halom spent part of Easter washing the players kit. His wife was not in favour of him using their own washing machine so he had to take shirts, shorts and stockings to the local launderette.

Promotion to the First Division for Wimbledon at the end of 1985–86 released their players from washing their own equipment. A washing machine company donated apparatus in recognition of their achievement.

In September 1982 Arsenal goalkeeper George Wood was given

the task of making a survey of winter birds in Great Britain, backed by the British Ornithological Trust.

On 29 September 1986, St Mirren captain Billy Abercromby, in his 12th year with the club, was shown the red card three times by referee Louis Thow in the match against Motherwell; the first for the dismissal, the second for talking out of turn, the third for dissent. He was given a 12 match ban, fined £500 by the Scottish Football Association and placed on the transfer list by manager Alex Miller.

Subsequently Miller left to take up an appointment with Hibernian and Alex Smith arrived from Stirling Albion as manager. Abercromby was back in the team by mid-January and on 16 May 1987 led St Mirren to success in the Scottish Cup, captaining them in a 1–0 win over Dundee United.

The two oldest clubs in existence, Sheffield and Hallam, met at Sandygate on Boxing Day 1985 to celebrate the start of Hallam's 125th birthday. Sheffield won 2–1. The first meeting between the two had been on Boxing Day 1860 when Sheffield won 2–0.

In 1984–85 Bernie Slaven scored 31 League and Cup goals for Albion Rovers and with his contract completed declined to re-sign for the club. Instead he waited for offers from other clubs. None arrived. So with the help of his mother and father he wrote to all 10 Premier Division clubs and the 44 English First and Second

Division clubs asking them to consider signing him. Eventually he was approached by Middlesbrough – from the Third Division – and he signed for them after a successful trial.

The final of the Colchester Challenge Cup in 1938 was played between Arsenal and Wolverhampton Wanderers. Both teams fielded a sprinkling of first team players and attracted a crowd of 17,584. Wolves won 1–0. At the time the Layer Road ground was unused to attendances of this size watching Colchester United.

John Shaw, Leeds United goalkeeper, was a Scottish schoolboy international at rugby and cricket and a juvenile international at basketball. He did not make any Football League appearances for the club before being transferred to Bristol City in May 1974 but had twice started matches in Europe, one in the Fairs Cup, the other in the UEFA Cup.

Walthamstow Avenue claim to possess the football world's only wooden cup. It was presented to them in the Second World War for a competition which they won regularly. It had been made from the mast of one of the small boats which ferried survivors in the Dunkirk evacuation in 1940.

On 9 May the last day of the 1986–87 League programme, three clubs, Burnley, Torquay United and Lincoln City, were vulnerable at the bottom of the Fourth Division. Whoever finished bottom would be automatically relegated to the GM Vauxhall Conference, the first time a club would lose its place in this way.

Burnley were at home to Orient who needed points themselves to qualify for a promotion play-off. The kick-off had to be delayed because of an unexpectedly large crowd. At Torquay the home side found themselves trailing 2–0 at half-time but pulled a goal back through Jim McNichol shortly after. Then in the dying minutes a police dog ran onto the pitch and bit McNichol. After the hold-up, Paul Dobson equalised in the last minute. Meanwhile Lincoln lost 2–0 at Swansea and with Burnley finally emerging 2–1 winners themselves, it was Lincoln who lost their League status despite spending just one minute during the entire season at the bottom of the table. On the Monday following the game, Torquay chairman Lew Pope bought 'Bryn' the police dog a large steak. Peter Daniel, the player-manager of Lincoln, was signed by Burnley for the following season.

In April 1986 Aldershot announced a £60,000 sponsorship over two years by a local car firm, TA Garages, whose managing director was a West Ham United supporter.

In February 1986, Middlesbrough offered Hartlepool United the use of Ayresome Park after the Division Four club were ordered to demolish two stands at the Victoria Ground for safety reasons. On 23 August 1986 Middlesbrough played their opening match of the season at Hartlepool because their own

ground had not been released by the official receiver following severe financial problems.

In March 1987 Stoke City revealed that their 21-year-old defender Chris Hemming was playing with a pacemaker fitted to his heart.

Tom Priestley is one of only two players to have worn a rugby scrum cap in the Football League, having lost his hair through a childhood illness. A Northern Ireland international inside-forward he was signed in June 1933 by Chelsea from Linfield for £2,000 after fierce competition from several other clubs, but stayed just one season at Stamford Bridge before returning to his native country. Though he never again participated in professional football he remained on Chelsea's retained list for several years. Steve Kindon wore a cap after a head injury while playing for Huddersfield Town in the 1970s.

In 1890–91 Chesterfield changed their colours from Cardinal and Sky Blue to Union Jack shirts.

When Berwick Rangers played Royal Oaks, a team of fishermen at Shieldfield in Tweedmouth, south of the river in 1890 it was a rough game. When the powerful Royal Oaks' centre forward broke through, he unnerved the Rangers goalkeeper by shouting: 'Cleghorn, if you stop the ball, I'll kill you.' It resulted in the only goal of the game.

Bury had scored only three goals in eight competitive games in 1981. Manager Jim Iley then decided on the extreme measure of dropping goalkeeper Neville Southall from training sessions because he was saving too many shots. In their next game Bury won 3–1.

Carlisle United once held the record for the oldest and youngest managers to have been put in charge of a Football League club for the first time. On 15 November 1975 Dick Young was appointed at the age of 58. In 1946 Ivor Broadis had been made player-manager when only 23.

In the 1967–68 season Ken Brown was a Torquay United half-back on Saturdays and the organiser of West Ham United's pools promotion scheme for the rest of the week.

In the post war period, Arsenal have supplied captains of all five countries in the British Isles: Alan Ball (England), Frank McLintock (Scotland), Walley Barnes (Wales), Terry Neill (Northern Ireland) and Liam Brady (Republic of Ireland).

Eighty-nine normal size walking steps separate the boundary wall of Dundee's Dens Park ground from that of Dundee United's Tannadice Park, the closest pair of senior clubs in British football.

Hereford United appointed Andy Feeley as captain during 1979–80

even though he was only 17 years of age. Port Vale had given Clint Boulton the same honour in 1964.

On the afternoon of Wednesday 19 March 1975, Russell Osman played for England schoolboys at rugby union against Wales at Twickenham and in the evening turned out for the Ipswich Town youth team against Arsenal.

In 1980 Prince Rainier of Monaco ordered shirts in Scotland's distinctive dark blue as family souvenirs. One had the number 20 and the name Rainier, the other 9 and Albert for his son.

In March 1959 Queens University won only their first match of the 1958–59 season in the 5–3 against Dundela Irish League B Division. But one of their supporters produced this list of results over the previous year to prove Queens to be as good as World Cup holders Brazil. Dundela drew with Glentoran 3–3; Glentoran beat Distillery 3–1; Distillery beat Linfield 1–0; Linfield drew with Newcastle United 3–3; Newcastle beat Wolverhampton Wanderers 2–1; Wolves drew with Hearts 1–1; Hearts beat the Scottish national team 3–2; Scotland beat Wales 3–0; Wales drew with England 2–2 and England drew wth Brazil 0–0.

Playing for Rotherham United against Bournemouth on 10 October 1972, Carl Gilbert scored both his team's goals in a 7–2 home defeat and then had three scored against him after he had become the emergency goalkeeper following an injury.

Brian Flynn scored in a full international for Wales v Scotland at Cardiff on 17 May 1965 and in a Football League Cup-tie for Burnley at Hereford on 9 September 1975 before he achieved his first goal in the Football League v Everton on 31 January 1976. He actually scored twice against Hereford.

In the 1946–47 season Scottish international inside-forward Tommy Walker played in 48 League games. After he had appeared in nine matches with Hearts in the Scottish League he moved to Chelsea and appeared in 39 in Division One.

In 1974–75 Dick Habbin played 27 games for Reading and a further 21 for Rotherham United after being transferred for a total of 48 Football League matches.

In 1986–87 Manchester City goalkeeper Eric Nixon made 44 League appearances for five different clubs. He was loaned to Wolverhampton Wanderers (16 appearances), Bradford City (3), Southampton (4) and Carlisle United (16) before being finally recalled to make the last five appearances of the season for his own club.

In 1967 Clydebank had the assistance of Ayrton Ignacio a Brazilian who had played for Celtic and Reims. In a match at Forfar it was so cold that he had to be substituted 15 minutes from the end of play.

The 'luck bringing' spats of Portsmouth manager Jack Tinn became famous in their 1939 FA Cup run, and Fred Worrall, the Pompey winger, had to fasten them on match days throughout the club's success that year. He became tired of the ritual but Tinn always insisted. Yet Worrall had his own superstition and always played with a sixpence (2½p) in his boot and a miniature horseshoe in his pocket.

Ben Beynon was the Welsh stand-off half against Scotland at rugby union on 7 February 1920 in Edinburgh and seven days later played as a professional for Swansea Town against Queen's Park Rangers at centre-forward.

Gareth Edwards, the former Welsh rugby international who signed Welsh League forms for Swansea City during the 1980–81 season, had been on the point of turning professional for Swansea when he was 17 years of age. He was an outside-left in the club's youth team but moved to Millfield School where he concentrated on rugby. In February 1981 he also signed non-contract forms for Swansea City in the Football League.

Dr Kevin O'Flanagan played for Ireland against France at rugby on 27 January 1946 in Dublin; for Ireland v Scotland at soccer the following week in Dublin and was chosen for Ireland v England at rugby again seven days later. But his train was late at Liverpool, he missed the boat to Dublin and was unable to travel by air thus missing a unique hat-trick. His brother Michael played centre-forward with Kevin at outside-right for the Republic of Ireland v England in Dublin on 30 September 1946.

H. W. Renny-Tailyour of the Royal Engineers played for Scotland at rugby union in 1872 and soccer in 1873, both times against England, and finished on the losing side on each occasion.

During the 1930s Celtic had a Swedish goalkeeper on their books called Julius Hjuliana, a Jewish player Jerry Solis and an Egyptian Abdul Salim who played several Alliance matches for the club with only bandages around his feet.

North Korea and South Korea have had virtually no contact with each other since the end of the Korean War in 1953. Yet in the 1980s they met each other in a match during the 17th King's Cup football tournament in Bangkok. There was

no incident during the game won by North Korea with a goal scored by Han Hyong II. He scored from a free-kick given for hands with a shot from 25 yards which was deflected into the goal after 32 minutes.

Stranraer's ground at Stair Park situated on the shores of Loch Ryan is on the same latitude as Newcastle and nearer to Ireland than Glasgow.

On 9 September 1916 2nd Lt Donald Bell, a Bradford Park Avenue back, became the only Football League professional in history to win the VC, awarded posthumously 'for most conspicuous bravery' on the Somme.

Robert Smith, a Welsh born referee who was employed as a railway shunter, had refereed only five Football League matches when he was appointed to control the Scotland v Ireland international at Hampden Park on 5 November 1952.

On 20 February 1982 the amateur match in the Scottish village of Fintry between Jack Scott Vics and Westburn had to be postponed. Officials arrived to find the ground under a massive deluge of molehills.

Hull City full-back Bobby McNeil began the 1981–82 season by being struck in the eye by a ball during training. His left eye was damaged

and he spent four days in hospital. The injury kept him out of action for six weeks. Then at Tranmere in February, he broke a bone in his left foot; only four comeback matches later he broke the same bone and at the end of the season he was given a free transfer.

On 26 March 1921 in a Division One match between Arsenal and Sheffield United there was a tussle close to the United goal-line between Dr Paterson (Arsenal) and Willie Cook the Sheffield full-back. The ball went over the line and the referee awarded a corner kick to Arsenal. However Dr Paterson walked across to the referee and protested that he had been the last to play the ball so the official changed his decision and awarded a goal kick.

Stirling Albion competed in the Scottish League Cup before they became members of the Scottish League. In 1945–46 they were included in Section D of the then Scottish Southern League Cup, qualifying competition, Division B and finished second to Dundee who were Division B champions that season.

Halifax Town, having been unable to play a home match since the previous 14 December because of frost and snow, made football history on 2 March 1963 when they opened their Shay ground to a paying public as an ice rink.

When Stewart McCallum played for Wrexham against Crewe Alexandra on 7 April 1951 he was under doctor's orders not to head the ball. Concussion sustained in a previous match was the reason for the strictness of this medical advice. In the 1970 World Cup, Brazilian striker Tostao was similarly warned after recovering from an operation for a detached retina in one eye.

The Football Association has never had a secretary who was born in the north, the Football League have never had one who came from the south.

The 1947–48 and 1962–63 seasons provided the post-war extremes in postponements due to adverse weather conditions. There were only six in the former season, but 307 in the other.

The Duncan Edwards Football Club, a memorial to the Manchester United and England half-back, who was a victim of the Munich air crash in February 1958, was formed in his native Dudley in September 1959. It was the only time a club has been named after a player. A stained glass window in Edwards' memory is also in the parish church of St Francis.

After Brazil's victory in the 1958 World Cup, their inside forward Didi had three streets and a railway station named after him . . . In the 1960s Swansea Town had an inside forward called Derek Draper who was known by his initials 'DD'. But his international career for Wales consisted of one Under 23 cap. Sir Stanley Matthews once had a British Rail carriage named after him.

KEEPING UP WITH THE...

In 1932–33 Wrexham had the following on their books: Albert Jones (full-back), J. R. Jones (right-half), F. W. Jones (left-half), Arthur Jones (right-wing), R. Jones (inside-right), Oswald Jones and Wilson Jones (both centre-forwards). The club's chairman was Dr Edward Jones. When local born Graham Jones signed professional forms for Wrexham at the age of 17 in October 1967, he became the 100th player with that surname to have been signed by the Racecourse Ground club since 1921.

effectively saved his life. Rogers was playing again in three weeks.

Charles Ford, a Scottish centre-forward making his Football League debut for Newcastle United v Grimsby Town on 16 January 1932, sustained a double leg fracture and never played in the competition again, though he resumed his career north of the border with Partick Thistle two years later.

Abide with Me was first sung at the FA Cup Final on the suggestion of Sir Frederick Wall, FA Secretary who wrote to King George V for permission to play it there, knowing it was the ruler's favourite hymn.

England played Argentina during their 1953 summer tour. The match began in torrential rain and had to be abandoned by referee Arthur Ellis after just 22 minutes. All the players were given full caps.

Among the footballers to whom the Freedom of the City has been granted have included: Kenny Dalglish (Glasgow), Sir Matt Busby (Manchester), Tom Finney (Preston) and Jackie Milburn (Newcastle).

After an accidental collision playing for Reading against Swansea City on 22 February 1986, Andy Rogers swallowed his tongue and actually stopped breathing for 90 seconds. Trainer Glenn Hunter plucked his tongue out with tweezers and

By 1962 inside-forward Nobby Lawton of Manchester United had already suffered double pneumonia, cartilage trouble, pleurisy, an appendicitis and a cracked shinbone. He was still only 22. But with United, Preston, Brighton and Lincoln his subsequent career produced over 300 League appearances.

CLASS OF '66

Twenty-one years after winning the World Cup in 1966 the successful England team were variously engaged as follows:

Gordon Banks	Public Relations, Leicestershire
George Cohen	Building and property
Ray Wilson	Undertaker
Nobby Stiles	Coach, West Bromwich Albion
Jack Charlton	Manager, Republic of Ireland
Bobby Moore	Football writer, *Sunday Sport*; Director, Southend United
Alan Ball	Manager, Portsmouth
Roger Hunt	Transport (haulage business)
Geoff Hurst	Car insurance
Martin Peters	Car insurance
Bobby Charlton	Travel business; coaching school; Director, Manchester United.

MONEY MATTERS

George 'Spry' Woodhall picked up £1 from West Bromwich Albion after their FA Cup Final win in 1888. His contract stipulated that he would be paid £1 for Saturday games, ten shillings (50p) for midweek matches. If required for midweek training he had to make himself available on Wednesday and Thursday afternoons without extra pay. The terms also insisted that he keep himself in good physical condition otherwise he would forfeit £1 a week.

Tottenham Hotspur almost lost their amateur status in their early years over a pair of football boots. They were due to play Old St Marks on 21 October 1893 in a London FA Cup tie with Eddie Payne about to make his debut for them. Payne, an outside left, had been rather neglected by Fulham during the previous season and had accepted Spurs' invitation to turn out for them. However, when he went to the Fulham ground to collect his gear he found that it had been stolen. Tottenham fixed him up with everything he needed except for a pair of boots. They gave him ten shillings (50p) to buy a pair.

After the match Fulham not only

complained that Spurs had poached their player but made a charge of professionalism in relation to Payne receiving money for the boots. The council of the London FA investigated the matter, and although they did not uphold the charge of poaching, as Fulham had not included Payne in their first team in any games the previous season, they did find that Spurs had broken the rules of amateurism in relation to the sum involved.

Spurs argued that the boots remained the property of the club and were not given to Payne but their argument was not accepted. Spurs were found guilty of misconduct. The club was suspended for a fortnight and Payne for one week. Payne retained his amateur status by repaying the club the ten shillings and eventually Tottenham turned professional themselves.

In 1881 two years after Sunderland had been formed they suffered a financial crisis which was saved by one of their members auctioning one of his prize canary pets. The bird and cage was raffled and fetched £1, which was enough to see them out of immediate fiscal embarrassment.

Albion Rovers chairman Tom Fagan bought 2,900 seats from the stand of the defunct Cathkin Park ground of Third Lanark in 1967. He resold 1,900 at a profit, installed 600 of the others in the stand at Cliftonville and utilised the remaining 400 for the balcony of the club house.

In October 1980 the Turkish Division One team Orduspor gave their goalkeeper Alptekin a £50 bonus for letting in four goals against Gaziantep. Handing over the money, the club chairman explained that he had expected to lose the game by at least double figures.

The 1979–80 season produced the first instances of a club making a million profit and another losing a similar amount. Nottingham Forest's profit was £1,258,000 while Manchester City lost £1,663,000.

In 1930 the referee's society passed a regulation that referees had the right to be paid match fees in their own dressing rooms. Previously they had had to run the gauntlet of disgruntled club managers refusing to pay the fees until asked and then only after giving the official a piece of their own mind over events during the match!

Only 2,000 turned up to see the first FA Cup Final at Kennington Oval when Wanderers beat Royal Engineers 1–0 in 1872. The admission price of one shilling (5p) was thought to be responsible for the poor attendance.

George Ross captained Bury from left-half in both their successful FA Cup winning teams of 1900 and 1903. He stayed 20 years with them until 1906 and an early reference in the club's minutes showed appreciation of his services: 'Resolved that the pay of George Ross be increased from three to four shillings (20p) per week.'

Alec Grant was probably the lowest paid professional footballer of all time *pro rata* when Derby County retained him at wages of 3d (1¼p)

a week in the 1947–48 season. A goalkeeper, he was also a schoolmaster at the time, taking examinations he had missed during the war, and agreed to this 'nominal' sum so that he could play when studies permitted.

Andy Graver was three times signed by Lincoln City and on each occasion he cost less money than when he had been transferred. He originally cost £3,000 when signed in September 1950 from Newcastle United. In December 1954 he went to Leicester City for £30,000; returned in June for £11,000; moved to Stoke City for £12,000 in November 1955 who sold him to Boston United for £4,000 in September 1957. Lincoln signed him for a third time in October 1958 for £1,500. And in 1964, three years after retiring, he became City's youth team coach.

When Arnaldo Coelho refereed the 1982 World Cup Final in Madrid he was reputed to be the world's highest paid referee at £500 a game. This Brazilian stockbroker from Rio de Janeiro lived overlooking the Copacabana Beach and trained there every day.

In February 1982 Chesterfield midfield player Geoff Salmons sacrificed three weeks wages voluntarily after being advised by a specialist to rest a hamstring injury.

Kenny Dalglish spent a fortnight on trial with Liverpool in 1966 while on the books of Celtic. He played for Liverpool's B team against Southport on 20 August 1966 wearing the No. 8 shirt in a match Southport won 1–0. He later returned to Celtic and was loaned to Cumbernauld. Liverpool eventually paid £440,000 for him in August 1977.

When Kuwait qualified for the 1982 World Cup finals in Spain, Crown Prince Sheik Saad Abdullah Al Sabah showered gifts on the players. The 24 man squad each received a Cadillac car, luxury villa, plot of land, gold watch and a speedboat.

On 20 April 1901 Tottenham Hotspur met Sheffield United in the FA Cup Final at Crystal Palace. Thomas Cook the travel agents offered a conducted drive, visiting principal places of interest in London in connection with Excursion trains being run to London by the Midland Railway. A meat breakfast was guaranteed on arrival, followed by the drive around London and dinner at the Crystal Palace. The inclusive charge of the day's outing was 6s. 6d (32½p).

The first player to score 200 post-war League goals was Wally Ardron who had actually started his Football League career with Rotherham United in 1938–39, making one appearance. They had signed him from Denaby United for £100 but finance of a more modest figure had nearly ended his career as a schoolboy in Swinton, Lancashire. His schoolmaster supplied the team with boots at six shillings (30p) a

pair which the players had to repay at 6d (2½p) a week. Ardron paid one shilling (5p) but found further payments a problem and decided to return the boots. The master told him to score three goals and he could keep the boots. He did.

In 1909 the finances of Cowdenbeath had reached such a low state that only the staging of whippet racing at their ground saved them from extinction. At that time an away tie in the Scottish cup proved an embarrassment through lack of funds, but the local station master turned a blind eye to their not having any train tickets.

On 2 September 1985 Trevor Senior scored a hat-trick for Reading at Cardiff only to be refused the gift of the ball by City manager Alan Durban, who, however, said he could have it for £40.

Colin Lister drew pay packets from six different clubs over a period of a year from 1963 to 1964: Bradford (Park Avenue), Bangor City, Bexley United, Gravesend and Northfleet, Boston United and Scarborough. He was 21 at the time.

In August 1985, Dundee United goalkeeper Hamish McAlpine, a three handicap golfer, played with Gordon McKay one hole on each of 50 different Scottish courses in a day to raise £1,000 for a child suffering from cerebral palsy. They started at 3.30 am and finished 19 hours later.

FOOTBALLING CLERGYMEN

The only occasion in Football League history of two clergymen playing together in the same side occurred in 1912–13 season when Wolverhampton Wanderers fielded the Rev. K. R. G. Hunt as a half-back and Rev. W. C. Jordan as a forward. Kenneth Hunt scored in the 1908 FA Cup Final for Wolves a week after assisting Oxford in the Varsity match against Cambridge. In 1903 he had played in the FA Amateur Cup Final for Oxford City. It is also accepted that he taught Charlie Buchan the art of positional play. The Rev. Norman Hallam was a methodist parson who played as a professional at wing-half for Port Vale and Halifax Town in the years immediately after the Second World War. Andrew Amos, who played twice for England in 1885–86, was ordained in 1887. In the post-war period Phil Gunter and Mike Tiddy were lay preachers and Dave Durie and Billy Liddell, Sunday school teachers, as well as professional footballers.

The referee in charge of the Division Two game between West Bromwich Albion and Blackpool on 3 December 1910 was the Rev. J. Marsh. One of his linesmen was the Rev. W. Strange.

On 24 August 1985 Hereford United's game with Swindon Town was sponsored by the Bishop, the Rt. Rev. John Easthaugh.

The following 'ecclesiastical' team has been drawn from Football League players past and present, under manager Dave Sexton.

Dennis Parsons	Wolverhampton Wanderers, Aston Villa
Fred Monk	Brentford, Aldershot
David Deacon	Ipswich Town
Greg Abbott	Bradford City
Sid Bishop	Orient
Philip Priest	Blackpool (on loan), Brentford (on loan)
Derek Temple	Everton, Preston North End
John Steeples	Grimsby Town, Torquay United (on loan)
Ian St John	Liverpool, Coventry City, Tranmere Rovers
John Church	Norwich City., Colchester United
George Prior	Newcastle United, Milwall

Substitutes: Mike Pentecost (Fulham), Paul Friar (Leicester City, Rotherham United, Charlton Athletic and Aldershot).

BELIEVE IT OR NOT

On 13 February 1982 Reading announced as an economy measure that the referee and linesmen at home matches would no longer be given biscuits at half-time. Nicknamed the Royals, Reading had previously been known as the Biscuitmen because of the close proximity of the Huntley and Palmers factory.

Athlone Town scored two goals in 13 seconds against Limerick without the opposition touching the ball. In a League of Ireland Shield game at St Mel's Park, Athlone, County Westmeath on 20 August 1972, Limerick won the toss and elected to kick-off. Three seconds before half-time, Athlone scored a goal. There was no time to re-start the match. After the interval Athlone kicked off and scored in ten seconds without a Limerick player touching the ball.

GETTING THERE...

In 1950–51 Rotherham United set off for a FA Cup tie at Darlington in a coach driven by Cyril Smart one of the club's directors. The registration number of the vehicle was GET 7. Rotherham won 7–2.

Benjamin Howard Baker was an England international goalkeeper while with Everton and Chelsea, Olympic athlete, Wimbledon tennis player, club cricketer, water polo international and accomplished sailor. He had competed in the 1912 and 1920 Olympics in the high jump and pentathlon and in 1921 won the British high jump championship at a record 6ft 5in. He used to swim 10–12 miles in the Mersey helping J. B. Crossley prepare for his Channel swims and also played rugby during his days in the RNVR in the First World War.

In October 1985 Mike Conroy was carried off with a leg injury playing for Blackpool against Bury which required eight stitches. Five weeks later he made a come back with the reserves against Sunderland but had to go off after an hour with a calf muscle strain. In December against York City reserves he lasted until half-time and the following day an x-ray revealed a broken bone in his right leg which had virtually healed itself, despite training and 105 minutes of football.

On 29 August 1987 Plymouth Argyle were fulfilling a Second Division fixture at Reading. A few minutes before half-time with the score 0–0, Argyle manager David Smith left the touchline dug-out and went to the dressing room to

organise refreshments. In his absence, the Reading defender Gary Peters put through his own goal to give Plymouth the lead. Unaware of this, Smith lectured the team during the interval, made two second half substitutions in frustration and at the final whistle still assumed the score was 0–0. It was several minutes into the after-match team talk that assistant manager Martin Harvey realised the situation and broke the good news to his manager. That win took Plymouth to the top of the division.

David Smith's playing career started with Ashdale Amateurs in Dundee. He later played for Dundee East Craigie, Burnley, Brighton and Hove Albion and Bristol City at full-back. He won Scottish Under-16 honours and was capped at amateur level. In 1953 he suffered a hair-line fracture of his right tibia. Three years later he had a hair-line fracture of his left fibula. During pre-season training at Burnley in 1959 he had a hair-line fracture of his left tibia and was out for 15 weeks only to suffer the same injury in training on his return. In 1961 he also had a hair-line fracture of his right fibula. But throughout his career he suffered no other injuries.

In 1958–59 Lincoln City had a 6ft 3in centre half called Ray Long and a 5ft 2in outside left called Joe Short who had a specially made kit.

During 1958–59, Coventry City had six goalkeepers on their staff: Jim Sanders, Arthur Lightening, Graham Spratt, Tom Brindley, Bob Wesson and Alf Wood. For part of the season the first choice was Wood, aged 42.

On 8 October 1983 Darlington midfield player Colin Ross lasted only five seconds against Chester. He injured his knee straight from the kick-off and was replaced by substitute Peter Cartwright.

In 1969–70, Rodney Marsh, Queen's Park Rangers forward, was given a permanent disability pension of 27 shillings (£1.35) as the result of deafness in one ear caused by heading the ball. The injury did not affect his career.

Jeff Taylor was a Huddersfield Town forward who had signed amateur forms for the club in the late 1940s while singing as a boy soprano at the local town hall. He was also studying geology and had ideas of becoming a teacher. He played for Huddersfield, then Fulham and Brentford before attending the Royal Academy of Music. His first professional engagement was with the Halle Orchestra and he also appeared at Glyndebourne. He used his middle name on stage, appearing as Neilson Taylor.

Bill Shankly's famous comment that football was more serious than life and death has not stopped several comedians joining the boards of Football League clubs. Those who have done so include: Tommy Trinder (Fulham), Eric Morecambe (Luton Town), Jasper Carrott (Birmingham City), Norman Wisdom (Brighton & Hove Albion), Charlie Williams (Barnsley), Tommy Cannon (Rochdale) and Jim Davidson (Bournemouth, Aldershot). Arthur English who had been an Aldershot director himself, became President of the club in 1986.

Forty years after it had been used in the 1928 FA Cup Final, the ball was still in the possession of Aussie Campbell, Blackburn Rovers left-half. He was working in a Blackburn brewery at the time.

England manager Bobby Robson was diagnosed to be suffering from tennis elbow on 12 February 1987, the result of an injury sustained playing golf.

On 8 October 1955 during the Third Division (Southern Section) match between Aldershot and Brentford, a small dog grabbed the flag carried by linesman Ronnie Chappell, ran off with it and disappeared.

Aberdeen's Belgian born goalkeeper Marc De Clerck scored a goal on his debut against Berwick Rangers in the Scottish League Cup on 30 August 1980 in the 22nd minute with a clearance which bounced over Berwick's centre-half and goalkeeper. De Clerck had been signed as cover for Bobby Clark, who in 1969 had for a time lost his first team place, but made an appearance as an outfield player as substitute against Rangers on 3 September 1969 and then in the No. 6 shirt against St Johnstone on 20 September.

Steve Murray was appointed manager of Forfar Athletic on 18 August 1980 and informed the club's board of directors that he was resigning on 21 August though the news was withheld from the playing staff until 23 August.

On 6 December 1952 the entire programme of matches in London had to be postponed because of fog when the games at Arsenal, Charlton Athletic, Chelsea, Brentford and Orient could not be played.

On 9 November 1980 Liberia played a goalless draw with Gambia in the Africa Cup and saved themselves from the firing squad. Known as the Lone Stars, the Liberian team had been threatened with execution by the Head of State if they failed to apply themselves well enough to the task.

The most appropriately named signing? Queen's Park Rangers apprentice Brian Inkpen in the 1965–66 season.

In August 1967 there was a junior game in Lisburn, Northern Ireland between Bridgeport and Collin Glen. The two teams arrived along with Jimmy Neill the referee and his two linesmen. But there was no match. Somebody had forgotten to bring the goalposts.

Alan Daley who up to December 1953 had played for nine different clubs inside and outside the Football League in a hectic spell of eight years, had previously been a runner with Mansfield Harriers.

Tim Ward was appointed manager of Exeter City in March 1953 but became manager of his former club Barnsley 25 days later. His actual stay at Exeter was only seven days because he was recalled by Barnsley who still held his registration as a player.

Bangor- born Steve Balcombe scored on his League debut for Leeds United against Aston Villa on 3 October 1981 in a 1–1 draw in Division One. He also made one substitute appearance for the Welsh Under-21 side against France in Troyes on 24 February 1982 in a goalless draw. He was given a free transfer at the end of the season and that ended his Football League career.

On 4 October 1913 in a Division Two match between Stockport County and Fulham, Norman Wood, the Stockport inside-left, headed through his own goal in the tenth minute in attempting to clear a corner kick to put Fulham ahead. Five minutes later he accidentally knocked the ball down with his hand in the penalty area and Fulham increased their lead from the resultant spot kick. Soon afterwards, at the other end, the Stockport inside-right was brought down in the area. Wood took the penalty kick but shot at the Fulham goalkeeper. Fulham won 3-1.

During the 1982–83 season Johan Cruyff took a penalty kick for Ajax against Helmond Sport. Instead of attempting a shot he tapped the ball to Jesper Olsen who in turn pushed it forward for Cruyff to score. Ajax, already a goal ahead, won 5-0.

Seven of Sunderland's regular team which was relegated from Division One for the first time in the club's history in 1958, subsequently became managers of Football League and non-league clubs: Stan Anderson, Billy Elliott, Billy Bingham, Don Revie, Alan O'Neill, Charlie Hurley and Amby Fogarty. Bingham (Northern Ireland) and Revie (England) later became national team managers.

Playing for Arsenal at Aston Villa in a Division One game on 14 December 1935, Ted Drake had eight shots at goal. He scored seven goals and hit the crossbar with his other attempt. Arsenal won 7-1.

After being admitted to the Football League in 1921 Southport never had a player sent off in a peace-time match in the competition until Walter Taylor, a back, was dismissed at Halifax on 18 October 1952. It was Southport's 1,027th Division Three (Northern Section) match.

Frank Saul's dismissal in a match at Burnley on 4 December 1965 ended the longest spell any club ever had without having a player sent off in a Football League peace-time match. Spurs' previous sending-off incident had occurred when Cecil Poynton was ordered off in a game at Stoke on 27 October 1928.

During the 20 seasons between the two World Wars the only Arsenal player ordered off in a Division One match was Welsh goalkeeper Dan Lewis in a game at Sunderland in April 1926.

In April 1952 Huddersfield Town were beaten 1-0 at Tottenham by a freak goal. Eddie Baily played the ball twice when taking a corner-kick. The referee had placed himself five yards from the flag and had been struck in the back by Baily's first kick before the Spurs player ran forward to centre the rebound which Len Duquemin headed into the net. Despite protests from the Huddersfield players the goal was allowed to stand. Huddersfield were relegated at the end of the season.

Carlisle United played cricket, Brighton displayed badminton and Bradford City indulged in hockey. Norman Cricket was a Carlisle player, Roger Badminton on Brighton books and Trevor Hockey similarly with Bradford City and several other clubs. But Orient are the only club to have played a banjo in a cup semi-final. Nigerian-born Tunji Banjo came on for them as substitute against Arsenal in 1978.

Two weeks before the start of the 1986–87 season, Reading's groundsman mistakenly sprayed neat weed killer on the pitch instead of a diluted solution. His name: Gordon Neate.

The shortest close season in Football League history extended for 70 days. The 1946–47 season continued until June 14 because of bad weather and the 1947–48 season started on 23 August.

During 1971–72, Hartlepool United used four different goalkeepers in four successive matches: Barry Noble, Mick Gadsby, Eddie Nisbett and Ron Hillyard, conceding respectively two, two, one and three goals in the process. At the end of the season the club had no professional goalkeepers on the staff. Hillyard had been on loan, Noble and Nisbett signed as amateurs and Gadsby was granted a free transfer.

In an episode of the BBC TV series *Dr Finlay's Casebook* which ran from 1959 to 1966, Alloa Athletic players took part in a football story involving Tannochbrae, the fictional local team. The leading role in the episode was taken by Brian Marjoribanks, a Hibernian forward and actor.

"HOORAY CHEER"

Wolverhampton Wanderers centre-forward George Hedley scored one of the team's goals in their 3–1 FA Cup Final win against Newcastle United in 1908. However, the effort split one of his boots which as a pair had 17 patches on them. Still he refused to part with them and declined to change into a new pair brought onto the field by the trainer.

IN POLE POSITION?

His Holiness Pope John Paul II was once a goalkeeper with the Polish amateur team Wostyla. In the immediate pre-war period the Polish international team had a forward named Hubert God.

In the 1961–62 season Millwall half-back Dave Harper sustained an injury which was not officially registered. Playing against Accrington Stanley he was so badly injured that he could not play again that season. But the Lancashire club resigned from the competition shortly afterwards and their record was expunged.

Officials of the Melgar club in Peru blamed the team's poor performances in the 1979 championship on witchcraft, exercised by a former member of the club against them. To counteract this, the players shirts were soaked in an anti-witchcraft herbal solution. Alas, Melgar finished bottom of the table. But in the play-offs, to avoid relegation among the bottom eight clubs, the spell worked and their final position was third.

Norwich City's Welsh international centre-half David Jones did not kick a ball in a first class match throughout the 1978–79 season after sustaining a serious knee injury, yet he was cautioned by a referee. It happened when referee Malcolm Sinclair booked him at a match against Ipswich Town because of comments he made as a spectator on the trainer's bench.

Oliver Cromwell presented the first cup which Sheffield Wednesday won. On 15 February 1868 Wednesday beat the Garrick Club in the final of the Cromwell Cup, a trophy presented by Oliver Cromwell, manager of the Alexandra Theatre.

In the years immediately following the Second World War on first team match days at the City Ground, Nottingham, a jackdaw boarded a Nottingham Corporation bus at Council House Square and alighted at Trent Bridge from whence he flew to the City Ground to watch Nottingham Forest. In 1986–87 a rabbit appeared at Stair Park, Stranraer to sit peacefully viewing home matches in the Scottish League, Division Two.

On 20 October 1928 Leicester City were playing Portsmouth in a Division One match. Arthur Chandler, the City centre-forward, had scored five goals when five swans flew over the ground at Filbert Street. Shortly afterwards a sixth swan crossed and Chandler soon added his sixth goal. Leicester won 10–0, their record score.

During the 1910–11 season, Morton players received an unusual offer from Duncan McPhail, a master butcher in Greenock, of a lamb to each player who scored a goal. At one stage several sheep were grazing at Cappielow Park. Centre-forward Tommy Gracie kept one which he christened Toby.

Malcolm MacDonald, Governor General of Kenya in the 1960s, was the son of Ramsay MacDonald, Prime Minister for three different periods from 1924–1935. Malcolm was invited to sign for Kingswood, a local Bristol club, and put his address on the registration form as No. 10 Downing Street.

Everton once had a 13–0 win at Prenton Park, the home of Tranmere Rovers. It was 22 July 1944 against Birkenhead. But the sport was baseball.

Playing for England against Scotland at Hampden Park in 1946, Denis Compton took a pass from Jimmy Hagan, ran down the wing, and crossed to Tommy Lawton who headed the ball over the bar. Compton fell after crossing and broke the corner flag at its base. A spectator emerged from the crowd snatched the post and vanished with it.

When goalkeeper Bill Allan joined Sheffield Wednesday in 1891 the club had no boots big enough to fit him. A cobbler in Sheffield worked through the night making him a special pair.

Sheffield Wednesday manager Derek Dooley went to work on Christmas Eve 1977 only to discover he had been sacked.

Adam Black, the Leicester City full-back who established a record number of League appearances for the club, married a girl of 17 when he was 58 . . . Raich Carter became a father at the age of 55.

MAGIC MAGYARS

Only one continental country has managed to score as many as six and seven goals against the full England team. Hungary achieved this feat twice in one season, winning 6–3 at Wembley and 7–1 in Budapest in the 1953–54 season. The interests of the team were as follows:

Gyula Grosics	Light music, literature
Jeno Buzanszky	Music, literature
Gyula Lorant	Light music, films
Mihaly Lantos	Light music, operettas
Jozsef Bozsik	Light music, films, soccer problems
Jozsef Zakarias	Opera, serious literature
Laszlo Budai	Films, adventure novels
Sandor Kocsis	Light music, operettas
Nandor Hidegkuti	Music
Ferenc Puskas	Art, ancient history
Zoltan Czibor	Historical films, novels.

GOOD NEWS...AND BAD

Chris Woods established a British record of over 13 matches (1,196 minutes) without conceding a goal before being beaten in the 70th minute of a Scottish Cup 3rd round tie against Hamilton Academical on 31 January 1987. Rangers lost 1–0.

Billy Minter scored seven goals for St Albans City against Dulwich Hamlet in a replayed fourth qualifying round FA Cup tie on 22 November 1922. Dulwich won 8–7. Minter later admitted that one of his goals had been scored by another St Albans player, 'Ginger' Figg!

On 21 December 1957 in a Second Division match, Huddersfield Town were leading 5–1 at Charlton with 20 minutes remaining. But they became the first team to score six goals and still lose a League match as Charlton won 7–6.

In 1946–47 Burnley played 51 League and Cup games and conceded only 32 goals. They did not let in more than two goals in any match, had 25 clean sheets and one spell of 38 games with just two defeats. But they finished second in Division Two and runners-up in the FA Cup to Charlton Athletic.

Of the goalkeepers registered by Football League clubs in the 1987–88 season only one, Jim Brown, had scored more than one goal in open play in first class football. In 1981 he had become the first goalkeeper in the NASL to score from a clearance playing for Washington Diplomats against Atlanta. On 8 October 1983 he celebrated a new one year contract with Chesterfield by scoring with a 96 yard clearance against Stockport County. In 1987–88 he was beaten ten times in a League game at Gillingham.

In 1985–86 Cardiff City assistant manager Jimmy Mullen introduced a series of pre-match exercises and

HOW WRONG CAN YOU BE...

Sunderland chairman Tom Cowie made this comment on Lawrie McMenemy's arrival as manager in 1985: 'He's arguably the best in the UK. The man is magic. Everybody loves him. He has charisma, ability and great personal charm. He has a command of the entire football situation.' In less than two years Sunderland had been relegated and McMenemy had resigned.

chants reminiscent of the New Zealand Rugby team as a measure to end a run of seven games without a win. It worked for five games in which Cardiff were unbeaten. But at the end of the season they were relegated.

In 1966–67 Clyde finished third in the Scottish League Division One behind Celtic and Rangers but were denied entry to the Fairs Cup because of the 'one city, one club' rule operating at the time.

In 1957–58 Manchester City scored 104 goals in Division One. They conceded 100. It is the only instance in Football League history of a club scoring and conceding a century of goals.

Halifax Town used both substitutes on 15 August 1987 in a Division Four match against Darlington and both Wayne Allison and Neil Matthews scored in the 2–2 draw. But Matthews' transfer from Grimsby Town had not been registered in time and subsequently Halifax lost the point by default.

Kazimierz Deyna celebrated his 100th appearance for Poland in a World Cup match against Argentina in the 1978 World Cup. He had a penalty kick saved and Argentina won 2–0.

Denis Law scored all six Manchester City goals in their 28 January 1961 fourth round FA Cup lead over

Luton Town. But at 6–2 the match was abandoned. City lost the replay 3–1, Law scoring for them.

Ray Yeomans captained Darlington when they won promotion in 1965–66 and was then given a free transfer at the age of 32. Nobody seemed interested in signing him so he thought of opening a butcher's shop. But Darlington offered him the position of coach and a year later he was appointed their manager.

George Raynor was a right-winger with Sheffield United, Mansfield Town, Rotherham United, Bury and Aldershot. Upon retiring he became Aldershot's reserve team trainer. He had a brief spell organising an international team in Iraq before becoming Sweden's national coach. They won the 1948 Olympic Games competition, were runners-up in the 1958 World Cup and finished third in both the 1950 World Cup and 1952 Olympics. In 1959 he was earning £5 a week as manager of Skegness.

Berwick Rangers goalkeeper Keith Davidson was voted the club's Footballer of the Year in the 1979–80 season. On 9 August 1980 he conceded nine goals at Hamilton Academical in a Scottish League, Division One match. The next Monday he was involved in an accident which wrecked his car; he lost his part-time employment as a draughtsman the next day and was dropped from the Berwick side on the following Wednesday.

Gordon Durie celebrated his 22nd birthday on 6 December 1987 by putting Chelsea ahead at Liverpool from the penalty spot in a Division One match, in the 22nd minute. Chelsea had not won a League game at Anfield since 1935 and had suffered 19 defeats and nine draws in the meantime. They still made it 20 defeats, losing 2–1.

Though Chester were beaten 7–0 at Wrexham in a Division Three (Northern Section) match on 25 April 1953, goalkeeper John Wright kept a clean sheet. Unfortunately he was carried off injured ten minutes after the kick-off and inside-right Ralph Morement had to deputise for him.

Wolverhampton Wanderers scored in 35 seconds in a Division One match at Southampton on 18 September 1965. Southampton won 9–3.

In the 1958–59 season, Aldershot established two club records. On 13 September they beat Gateshead 8–1 for their highest League win and on 25 October at Hartlepool they scored in six seconds through Albert Mundy. At the end of the season they had to seek re-election.

Fred Fox was selected to play for England against France in May 1925 while a Gillingham player. But by the time the match was played he had been transferred to Millwall. A goalkeeper, he actually only appeared in the first half in Paris on 21 May before being kicked in the

face. Billy Walker took over in goal in the second half but England still won 3–2 with ten men.

On 2 September 1939 Bournemouth beat Northampton Town 10–0 at Dean Court. The following day war was declared.

Doncaster Rovers created several club and Football League records in the 1946–47 season: 72 points; 33 wins including 18 away; only three defeats; an intact defensive record in 20 matches and 42 goals for Clarrie Jordan at centre-forward. The following season they were relegated.

On 27 November 1916 a doomed German Zeppelin, caught in the glare of searchlights and in flames from the fire of a persistent Royal Flying Corps pilot's armoury, jettisoned its remaining bombs as it made for the sea. Two of them shattered the main stand at Hartlepool United's ground. After the war the club claimed £2,500 compensation from the German government. The claim was relentlessly pressed by correspondence, but the only tangible reply was another bomb in the vicinity during the Second World War.

In the 1938–39 season Doug Hunt scored 24 League goals for Sheffield Wednesday and Gilbert Alsop equalled this figure for Walsall. Hunt's best performance was scoring six of the seven goals by which Wednesday beat Norwich

City on 19 November in a Division Two match. Alsop had a spell in which he scored 4, 2, 3, 3, 4 and then all four goals in an FA Cup replay against Notts County. Wednesday missed promotion by one point and Walsall finished second from bottom in Division Three (Southern Section) and had to seek re-election.

Bristol City's first goal in Division One for 65 years was scored by Paul Cheesley in August 1976 in a 1–0 win against Arsenal at Highbury. It was Cheesley's last League goal before a knee injury led to the premature end of his League career.

On 1 February 1936, 209 goals were scored in the Football League; 46 in Division One, 46 in Division Two, 49 in Division Three (Southern Section) and 68 in Division Three (Northern Section). But in the Southern Section, Aldershot and Bristol City featured in the only goalless draw.

In 1978–79 Stuart Robertson, the Northampton Town central defender, was voted Player of the Year by the club's supporters. A week later he was given a free transfer.

Universidad de Nuevo Leon won the 1981–82 Mexican Division One title, beating Atlante 3–1 on penalty kicks after the two-legged play-off

had finished all square. But the club's Uruguayan coach Carlos Miloc had to watch the final stages in the dressing-room on television as he had been sent off from the touchline for protesting to the referee.

A local garage group offered a car worth £3,500 to any Crewe Alexandra player who scored 30 League goals in the 1982–83 season. Crewe's entire output in Division Four during 1981–82 had been 29.

Harry Woodhouse studied music and learned to play the violin, eventually reaching a standard whereby he was able to attend the Royal College of Music at Manchester. He progressed so well that he completed a season's engagement with the Halle Orchestra under the baton of Sir John Barbirolli. He combined his musical talents with football and on 19 August 1950 made his debut for Aldershot 'A' team against Eastleigh Spartans and had scored a hat trick when he had the misfortune to break his leg. He was unable to train until February 1951 and was almost immediately called up for Z training in the army. At the end of the season he was given a free transfer.

Stuart McManus, 20, scored on his debut for Southampton against Queen's Park Rangers on 11 March 1986. The following month he was given a free transfer.

DEGREES OF SUCCESS

Argentina's 1978 World Cup winning squad of 22 players had varied stages of educational status.

Name	Educational stage reached
Norberto Alonso	Primary
Osvaldo Ardiles	University
Hector Baley	Primary
Daniel Bertoni	Primary
Ubaldo Fillol	Primary
Americo Gallego	Primary
Luis Galvan	Secondary
Ruben Galvan	Primary
Rene Houseman	Primary
Mario Kempes	Secondary
Daniel Killer	Primary
Omar Larrosa	Primary
Ricardo La Volpe	Secondary
Leopoldo Luque	Primary
Jorge Olguin	Primary
Oscar Ortiz	Primary
Miguel Oviedo	Primary
Ruben Pagnanini	Secondary
Daniel Passarella	Primary
Alberto Tarantini	Secondary
Daniel Valencia	Primary
Ricardo Villa	Primary

WHAT'S IN A NAME?

Early in the second half of an FA Cup second round tie against Nuneaton Borough on 20 November 1971, Torquay United withdrew ex-Coventry defender Brian Hill. His substitute was the unrelated former Bristol City winger Brian Hill.

A pre-war West Bromwich Albion centre-half was christened Arthur Griffith Stanley Sackville Redvers Boscawen Trevis. He made only one League appearance for WBA before moving to Chester. In the post-war period Arsenal and Manchester United had a centre-half just called Ian Ure.

Barnsley referee Keith Styles named his house 'Nay-Ref', Leo Callaghan the Welsh referee called his 'Offside', Mike Kerkhof (Bicester) gave his tag 'Goal', Jim Finney went continental in his naming of 'Arbitro' and George McCabe (Sheffield) decided to commemorate being selected to control matches in the 1966 World Cup by calling his dwelling 'Jules Rimet' after the trophy itself.

Plymouth Argyle had one of the few black players on the staffs of Football League clubs between the two World Wars. He was Jack Leslie an inside-forward. His wing partner was Scottish-born Sammy Black.

Several times in the mid-1950s the Danish national team included the following: Rich Moller Nielsen, Verner Nielsen, Erling Nielsen, Flemming Nielsen, Hans C. Nielsen and Ove Bech Nielsen.

In 1932–33 Grimsby Town had two Charlie Wilsons on their staff. In 1949–50 Bradford City had two players by the name of Johnny Millar, both Scots. They frequently drew each other's pay by mistake. In the immediate pre-war period Newport County signed two players called Bill Owen. Neither had another initial, so a local newspaper decided to add a fictitious one to

WHO'S BEST...

In 1969–70 four countries considered that they had the 'best' player in the world. Northern Ireland's George Best with Manchester United; English-born David Best with Ipswich Town; Scot Billy Best with Southend United and Bermuda-born Clyde Best at West Ham United.

each, giving the former Exeter City player an 'E' and the ex-Manchester City one an 'M'. And as WE and WM they remained during their careers.

Bill Burnicle was a pre-war Football League professional and post-war manager and coach in England, Sweden, Sudan and Chile. It was only when he stopped playing that he revealed his real name was Burnikell. In his last season as manager of Tottenham Hotspur, manager Peter Shreeves insited his name had been Shreeve all along.

In the 1949–50 season, Leslie, Herbert, Antony and Jeff Smith were Aston Villa players, Bill Smith secretary and Norman and Edward Smith directors.

In 1966–67 Chester's playing staff included seven of the Jones boys: Bryn, Les, Ray, Howard, Bobby, David and Keither.

Two players both named Francis Lee studied together at Horwich Technical College in Lancashire and formed the right wing in the same side. Both later became professionals with Lancashire clubs, Preston North End and Bolton Wanderers, and both had trials with Lancashire County Cricket Club.

In the 1950–51 season Rotherham United ran four teams and each was captained by a Williams; the first by Horace, the second by Danny, the third by Ken and the fourth by Bobby. They were not related.

Robin Friday became a professional with Reading on Tuesday 22 January 1974 and made his debut on Sunday 10 February against Exeter City.

When Aston Villa first entered the FA Cup in the 1879–80 season they were drawn away to Stafford Road Railway Works, the leading Wolverhampton club at the time. Villa drew 1–1 and won the replay 3–2 at Perry Barr. They were drawn against Oxford University in the second round but withdrew. While the Varsity were formidable at the time it seems more probable that Villa's Birmingham Senior Cup tie with Birmingham was more important to them and they won the trophy that season.

Neville Ross gave his son the following names after Liverpool's 1974 FA Cup final win over Newcastle United: Kevin Stephen Emlyn Alexander Philip Peter Thomas Ian John Raymond Brian William (after Bill Shankly) Ross. Gwyn Edwards gave his daughter their second names: Victoria Shankly Clemence Smith Lindsay

Thompson Cormack Hughes Keegan Hall Heighway Toshack Callaghan Lawler Edwards.

In April 1966 Peter O'Sullivan, then a 35-year-old bricklayer and a Liverpool supporter, went to a local registry office and had his newly-born daughter officially named: Paula St John Lawrence Lawler Byrne Strong Yeats Stevenson Callaghan Hunt Milne Smith Thompson Shankly Bennett Paisley O'Sullivan.

To commemorate England's World Cup triumph in 1966 Peter Eastaway named his son Peter Derek Banks Cohen Wilson Stiles Charlton Moore Ball Hurst Hunt Peters Ramsey Eastaway.

Michael Sutton gave his son a similar list to commemorate Liverpool's 1973 League championship and UEFA Cup successes. The youngster was named: Kirk Lee Keegan Heighway Cormack Toshack Hughes Callaghan Hall Lloyd Smith Lindsay Lawler Clemence Shankly Sutton.

Even Charlton Athletic's team of the early 1970s was not forgotten by Mrs Linda Neighbour: Baby John Robert Philip Peter David Vincent Colin Michael Paul Arthur Keith Theodore (Theo Foley, Charlton's manager) Neighbour.

In November 1958 Gateshead signed Ken Smith from Shrewsbury Town. He was a forward and the club already had a Ken Smith on their books signed from Blackpool in August 1952. Neither had another initial so the original was called Ken Smith No. 1 and the newcomer Ken Smith No. 2.

In 1962 Dundee United had two players called Eric Brodie and luckily one had an additional initial 'S' to keep them separate. In the 1960s St Mirren solved the problem of two Bobby Campbells by naming one Red Campbell and the other Black Campbell.

In August 1987 Aldershot signed a left-back called David Barnes from Wolverhampton Wanderers. They already had a David O. Barnes on their staff who was a right-winger. But the forward had always been known as Bobby. Left-back Barnes dislocated his shoulder shortly afterwards and during his injury absence, Bobby Barnes was transferred to Swindon Town. When fit again David's first game was strangely enough in Bobby's former No. 7 shirt.

Chelsea had two goalkeepers called Bill Robertson on their books between July 1946 and December 1948, although William Gibb Robertson did not make his first team debut until William Harold Robertson had been transferred away from the club.

IF THE NAME FITS

Over the 100 years of the Football League the most appropriately-named players could have made up this team:

Keith Ball	Walsall, Port Vale
Nick Marker	Exeter City, Plymouth Argyle
Tony Goodgame	Orient
Tommy Fairfoul	Liverpool
Bob Scorer	Hull City, Bristol Rovers
Dennis Thrower	Ipswich Town
Fred Forward	Crystal Palace, Newport County, Portsmouth, Hull City
Frank Shooter	Notts County
Ted Passmore	Swansea Town, Gateshead
Norman Corner	Hull City, Barrow, Lincoln City, Bradford City
Tony Field	Halifax Town, Barrow, Southport, Blackburn Rovers, Sheffield United.

Substitutes: Roy Player (Grimsby Town, Oldham Athletic), Sidney Atack (Halifax Town).

THE NUMBERS GAME

In 1938–39 Walter Hunt scored four, four and three goals in Division Three (Northern) matches for Carlisle United respectively against Lincoln City, Accrington Stanley and Rochdale, the three clubs in question having been his former teams.

West Ham United centre-forward Vic Watson scored a club record 42 League goals in the 1929–30 season. He was particularly harsh on Leeds United with nine of the ten West Ham goals in two League games and one FA Cup match. He scored all four in the cup and a hat-trick in the home League match while some sources credit him with the own goal which deprived him of a hat-trick at Elland Road in the away fixture.

In the strict sense of the word the number of 'caps' awarded to players in the British International

Championship between 1953 and 1984 is misleading. On 29 August 1953 the four British national associations decided that each player who participated in British International Championship matches would receive one cap for each series rather than one for each actual appearance.

Thus for example Billy Wright who appeared in 18 Championship games after the date mentioned, received only a further six 'caps'. He had previously won 20 Championship caps and in his overall career 67 caps against foreign opposition. Thus his 105 'caps' were strictly only 93!

In April 1986 Brechin City goalkeeper Derek Neilson had completed a marathon of 50 visits to the dentist over a year following a serious facial injury in a match against Ayr United. He had lost three front teeth, had two back teeth shattered and 27 stitches in his jaw. The dentist had to rebuild his back teeth using pure gold.

West Ham United goalkeeper Peter Grotier was only 18 years of age when he turned out for four different teams in five matches over a period of eight days in April 1959. Successively he played in the 'A' team, reserves, youth side, reserves again and then made his first team debut.

Chesterfield travelled to Gillingham for a Third Division game on 5 September 1987 having not conceded a goal in 360 minutes of League football from the start of the season. Their hosts Gillingham

had failed to score in their only two matches. The result: Gillingham 10 Chesterfield 0. It was Gillingham's highest victory and Chesterfield's heaviest defeat and though they were handicapped by an injury to goalkeeper Jim Brown in the early stages they did not replace him.

Winger Terry Curran, who became known by his initials 'TC', had the wanderlust in his early years after leaving school and in three years had 13 different jobs. After turning to professional football with Doncaster Rovers he subsequently played for Bury (on loan), Nottingham Forest, Derby County, Southampton, Sheffield Wednesday, Sheffield United, Everton, Huddersfield Town, Hull City, Sunderland, Panionios and was with Grimsby Town and Chesterfield in 1987–88.

Ali Bin Haji Ismail, only 5ft 6in, made his debut in goal for Brunei at the age of 16 and let in seven goals against Thailand. But he went on to play 125 times for his country before becoming a Physical Education student at Jordanhill College, Glasgow at the age of 30. In his first game for them he let in seven goals.

Celtic were the last of the Scottish League clubs to wear numbers. They first wore them on their shorts in a friendly against Sparta Rotterdam in May 1960 and celebrated with a 5–1 win.

Between 1975–76 and 1985–86 Football League attendances

throughout the competition were reduced by a third from 24.8 million to 16.4. But for the 15 clubs in the Midlands the loss was half with only Nottingham Forest showing an increase:

Nottingham Forest	+29%
Port Vale	−11
Walsall	−19
West Bromwich Albion	−27
Chesterfield	−32
Coventry City	−41
Leicester City	−48
Derby County	−52
Mansfield Town	−52
Notts County	−59
Aston Villa	−60
Birmingham City	−60
Stoke City	−63
Lincoln City	−72
Wolverhampton Wanderers	−79

When Chelsea had Billy 'Fatty' Foulke playing in goal for them at 6ft 3in and 22st 3lb they used to call attention to his bulk by sending two small boys out with him to stand behind his goal. They became the forerunners of the first ball boys. Foulke's jersey was three times ordinary size.

In 1925–26 England beat Wales 3–1 and seven of that team did not play again that season for the national side. The team which drew 0–0 with Ireland had nine changes and for the match with Scotland seven new players appeared. This made 28 players for 33 positions in an unbeaten run. A friendly in which Belgium were beaten 5–3 gave eight others one game only. Overall seven players won their only international cap.

Fifteen of the 19 players used by Northampton Town in 1975–76 scored goals from a penalty kick, including goalkeeper Alan Starling. The total number of appearances made by the four who did not find the net came to just 16, including one substitute appearance and three full games by the other goalkeeper used.

Yorkshire born Republic of Ireland international Mick McCarthy was with Manchester City in the First Division in 1985-86. In the previous five seasons he had been with City in Division Two, Barnsley in Division Two, Three and Four.

On 21 May 1963, Chelsea won promotion to Division One by beating Portsmouth 7-0 at Stamford Bridge on goal average from Sunderland. They were runners-up with a goal average of 1.928 compared with Sunderland's 1.527. In the previous match they had won 1-0 at Sunderland.

Everton became the first Football League club to reach 3,000 matches in Division One, when they visited Brighton and Hove Albion on 7 October 1980. The Brighton directors presented their Everton counterparts with an engraved tray to commemorate the occasion. Everton won 3-1.

NO TEA PARTY...

After Aldershot had been beaten 9-2 away to Clapton Orient in a Division Three (Southern Section) match on 10 February 1934 the vanquished team took afternoon tea in a local hotel. The head waiter reported to the director in charge of the Aldershot party of 20 that he had laid 'nine on one side, nine on the other, with the remaining two, one at each end . . .'

Towards the end of the 1935-36 season Blackburn Rovers were forced to field five different goalkeepers in a run of nine games over six weeks, because of a series of injuries, and were relegated from the First Division.

On 5 September 1896 Blackburn Rovers met Liverpool in a Division One match during which seven goals were scored but only one was allowed. Blackburn had the ball over the line five times, three goals were disallowed for offside, another because the referee had blown for half-time and finally the one that counted. Liverpool had both their efforts ruled out, one for offside and the other from an indirect free-kick which went in without the ball touching another player. In the Division Three match between Swindon Town and Southend United which ended in a 2-2 draw on 5 November 1949, six goals were disallowed, all for offside, four of them netted by Swindon.

Dave Easson scored a club record 45 League goals for Arbroath in 1958-59 without any other player in the club reaching double figures.

Albert Juliussen brought up in Northumberland of Norwegian extraction made his debut for Huddersfield Town during the last war. While serving in the Army he played in a service game and scored six goals in the first half. He swapped sides after the interval and scored five times but finished on the losing side. After the war he had the distinction of scoring six goals for Dundee on 8 March 1947 against Alloa Athletic in a Division Two game and on 22 March he scored seven against Dunfermline Athletic.

In ten seasons from the start of the Apprentice scheme in the Football League in 1960, 2,126 youngsters were signed by League clubs and 1,157 of them went on to sign full professional forms.

Chesterfield's opponents in the FA Cup's first two rounds in the 1960–61 season were Doncaster Rovers and Oldham Athletic, and so they were again a year later! The mathematicians at Manchester University assessed the odds against such a double coming up as 3,081 to one.

During Accrington Stanley's last season in the Football League in 1961–62 the club sent a letter to Sylvester Bickerton of Padiham, inviting him to a trial. Sylvester was 71.

Stirling Albion failed to score any goals in the last 13 matches of the 1980–81 season.

Nigerian centre-forward Tesi Balogun was born in Lagos and played for Peterborough United, Skegness and Queen's Park Rangers after a trial. Ten years later he wrote to Rangers from Nigeria, asking his former club to check his date of birth.

On 15 August 1981 Fijian goalkeeper Akuila Nataro Rovono conceded seven first half goals to New Zealand in a World Cup qualifying match. He was replaced during the interval by Semi Bai who let in six. Two days earlier Fiji had lost 10–0 to Australia.

In the 1981–82 season the League of Ireland introduced a new points system awarding four for an away win, three at home, two for an away draw and one at home. The League was sponsored by Kentucky Fried Chicken.

Leeds United achieved or equalled nine club records in 1968–69: most points 67; most home points 39; most wins 27; most home wins 18; fewest defeats two (both away, another record); unbeaten at home; 26 goals conceded: nine conceded at home.

In 1980–81 Southend United established 17 club records. They recorded 42 home points; 30 wins including 19 at home ; 18 successive home wins; 15 successive home wins from the start of the season; 32 unbeaten home games; 31 goals against; 11 away wins; 25 clean sheets (including 17 at home, 10 of them successively); 10 'doubles' against other teams; six goals against at home (a Division Four record); goalkeeper Mervyn Cawston completed 985 minutes without conceding a goal at home between August and December; they were undefeated throughout the season at home; had fewest defeats in a season; and no team completed the 'double' against them. The club were Division Four champions.

Only 983 spectators watched the European Championship match between the USSR and Finland in the 103,000 capacity Lenin Stadium in Moscow on 31 October 1979. The temperature was 10 degrees below freezing and several players wore tracksuit trousers and bobble hats. The match ended in a 2–2 draw.

In 1972–73, Walsall established a post-war record in using seven different goalkeepers in League games. Bob Wesson appeared in 23 Division Three games, Dennis Peacock in ten, Glen Johnson, John Osborne and Ian Turner three each and Keith Bell and Jimmy Inger two each.

Aberdeen, pioneers of the first-all-seated stadium in the British Isles at Pittodrie, introduced numbers on the front of their players' shirts in the 1967–68 season in the same manner as American 'Gridiron' footballers uniforms.

In the first 20 years of the Maracana Stadium in Rio de Janeiro more than 58 million spectators watched 1,823 matches in the world's largest arena built for the 1950 World Cup with a capacity of 200,000. A revised attendance figure of 173,830 paying customers was given for the Brazil v Uruguay World Cup Final in 1950 but was twice topped: 177,656 for a Carioca championship match between Flamengo and Fluminense and 183,341 for a World Cup preliminary match between Brazil and Paraguay in '69.

Year	Spectators	No. of matches
1950	1,623,908	54
1951	2,953,136	82
1952	2,486,160	78
1953	2,898,554	90
1954	2,514,619	83
1955	2,721,403	90
1956	3,262,153	88
1957	2,338,686	92
1958	2,426,715	85
1959	2,317,284	84
1960	2,197,793	82
1961	2,239,813	84
1962	2,285,627	78
1963	2,442,926	89
1964	2,308,850	93
1965	3,382,382	102
1966	1,913,315	69
1967	2,280,932	92
1968	4,301,531	99
1969	4,902,862	98
1970	4,383,354	111

By the age of 21 in January 1987, Keith Wright, who had just signed for Dundee, had already played under seven managers. He first signed 'S' forms for Hibernian manager Eddie Turnbull. During his first year Willie Ormond took over there and was followed by Bertie Auld. He dispensed with the 'S' signings and Wright went back to minor soccer, until Gordon

Wallace signed him for Raith Rovers. A week later Wallace went to Dundee United and Raith's next two managers were Bobby Wilson and Frank Connor. Number seven, Jocky Scott paid £50,000 to take him to Dens Park, Dundee.

Pele scored his 1,000th first class goal in 1969. His year by year total in all games was:

1956	2	1963	82
1957	65	1964	62
1958	83	1965	107
1959	125	1966	40
1960	74	1967	53
1961	107	1968	39
1962	97	1969	64
Total	1,000		

On 4 October 1952, Bradford City's forward line against Darlington was Don Woan 5ft 7in, Jim Anders 5ft 3½in, Eddie Carr 5ft 6in, Whelan Ward 5ft 2¾in and Arthur Kendall 5ft 6in. In 1956 Burnley's regular forward line consisted of Billy Gray 5ft 6in, Bobby Burke 5ft 4in, Peter McKay 5ft 5in, Bert Cheeseborough 5ft 6in and Brian Pilkington 5ft 7in.

Ronnie Allen scored goals in more senior football seasons than any other player. He completed 19 peacetime seasons 1946–47 to 1964–65 as well as 1944–45 and 1945–46, respectively the war and transitional season.

In 1954 Thatcham beat Newbury Boys Club 43–0. Everybody in the team scored once while the goalkeeper hit two. Eight other goals were disallowed.

Goalkeeper Ted Burgin suffered a broken arm on nine occasions, a fractured leg twice, cracked ribs and a broken collar-bone, but still managed to play in Sheffield United, Doncaster Rovers, Leeds United and Rochdale more than 500 League games and appear twice for the England 'B' team.

On 4 December 1982 in the sixth minute of the Leicester City v Fulham match, four different footballs were used in a 30-second spell. The first was kicked out of the ground and two others were rejected as too soft by the referee.

Walter Robbins, Cardiff City's Welsh international forward, scored his 37th goal at Brentford in February 1932. It was the first he had scored anywhere except on his home ground Ninian Park.

When Barnsley won the FA Cup in 1911–12 they played 12 matches and had 20 hours of football. Half of their games ended in goalless draws.

During 23 years with Hull City up to December 1961 goalkeeper Billy Bly sustained 13 fractures to hands, feet, legs and ribs. Stoke City centre-half Denis Smith suffered five broken legs, four broken noses, a cracked ankle, broken collar-bone, chipped spine, countless broken fingers and toes plus over 100 stitches.

SOCCER AND SHOW BUSINESS

The halcyon days of the Show-Biz XI were in the late 1950s and early 1960s. Frequent televised matches featured them in the days before Football League and cup games appeared on the small screen. Among the regular players were Sean Connery in his pre-James Bond 007 era and Des O'Connor the singer. O'Connor had been evacuated to Northampton during the war and played for Northampton Town youth team.

In reverse roles players like Colin Grainger of Sheffield United and England, Cliff Portwood of Preston North End, Port Vale, Grimsby Town and Portsmouth were more than useful singers while Terry Venables sang with the Joe Loss Orchestra.

Other show business personalities have had strong links with the game. Richard Attenborough, the film actor and director, was on Chelsea's board at one time. International TV personality David Frost was on Nottingham Forest's wanted list as a youth.

Spanish singing star Julio Iglesias played for Real Madrid's youth team while studying law at Madrid University. His playing career was wrecked by a car accident.

HOWLERS

In October 1982 Jorge Nino scored three of Atletico Mineiro's goals in a 5–1 win over Democrata, eliminating the latter team from the Minas Gerais State Championship in Brazil. Unfortunately, Nino was a member of the Democrata club and his hat trick came from a trio of own goals.

On 4 March 1972 Tommy Wright put through his own goal after 35 seconds of Everton's Mersey derby with Liverpool. The following Saturday he repeated the error against Manchester City in another First Division match after just 32 seconds.

On 18 December 1954 Leicester City defenders Jim Milburn and Jack Froggatt were involved in a misunderstanding in front of their own goal in a Division One match against Chelsea at Stamford Bridge. They went for the ball together and

connected with it simultaneously, sending it into their own goal. It went into the records as 'Milburn and Froggatt shared one own goal'. Chelsea won 3–1.

In 1955 John Sillett was a 19-year-old full-back with Chelsea who received his calling-up papers for National Service. Unfortunately he had already been serving in the Army for ten months at the time.

Dennis Evans, 16, making his debut in goal for Gorleston against Gillingham in an FA Cup tie in November 1957, was on the losing side in a 10–1 defeat.

When Plymouth Argyle met West Ham United at Upton Park on 16 October 1936 their manager Robert Jack protested after the kick-off that the West Ham goalkeeper was wearing a green jersey which clashed with Argyle's shirts.

Pat Kruse put through his own goal while playing for Torquay United

WHISTLER'S BOTHER...

On 17 December 1955 at Highbury, Arsenal left-back Dennis Evans on hearing a whistle thought it was the end of the game. He flicked the ball casually into his own net only to discover it came from the crowd and the referee awarded a goal as the match with Blackpool was still on. But Arsenal won 4–1.

against Cambridge United on 3 January 1977. Time: eight seconds.

Jimmy O'Neill made his international debut in goal for the Republic of Ireland against Spain in Madrid on 1 June 1952. He found himself beaten twice before he touched the ball at all and once again before he had the opportunity of making any kind of save. Spain won 6–0.

On 18 October 1981 two teams arrived at Queen of the South's

ground at Palmerston Park for a reserve match. Morton's second team thought they were playing the Dumfries club in a Reserve League game and Southern Counties side, Threave Rovers, had arrived for a Challenge Cup tie. In the event Queen's played Morton and Threave sat it out.

Between 1937 and 1947 Mansfield Town operated in Division Three (Southern Section), while Crewe Alexandra were members of Division Three (Northern Section). But Mansfield is some 20 miles north of Crewe.

Southampton defender Tony Byrne received his first Republic of Ireland international cap 18 years after winning it. He was 40 at the time and had been forced into premature retirement from the

game through an arthritic knee. The cap was sent through the post not to Hereford where he lived, but to Hertford.

Playing for Sheffield Wednesday against Lincoln in 1888, Tom Cawley, who had an exemplary record of discipline, was sent off in error by the referee. Realising his mistake almost immediately the official called Cawley back but the player refused to return on a matter of principle.

On 9 December 1961 the Watford v Grimsby Town game came to a dramatic halt when a two-foot hole suddenly appeared near the penalty spot of the visitor's goalmouth at Vicarage Road. The game was held up for ten minutes while extra turf was cut away from the surrounds of the pitch and the hole was filled in.

SOCCER AND THE SILVER SCREEN

TRANSFERS OF DELIGHT

Harry Jackson, a centre-forward, was transferred on successive Christmas Eves: in 1947 to Preston North End from Manchester City and on to Blackburn Rovers in 1948.

Swansea Town centre-forward George Lowrie was transferred to Preston North End on 21 December 1937 for a fee and two players in exchange: Leslie Vernon and Joe Beresford. Lowrie was only 18 years of age at the time.

Uruguayan First Division club Rentistas wanted to sign Daniel Allende from Second Division Central Espanol in 1979 but had no money. However their President owned a slaughter house and he agreed to allow Espanol to receive 550 beef steaks for the player at the rate of 25 a week plus 30 per cent of any subsequent transfer fee.

Tommy Tynan signed apprentice forms for Liverpool on his 16th birthday on 17 November 1971. He had been spotted by Bill Shankly in the finals of a competition organised by the *Liverpool Echo* and which had an entry of 1,000. Tynan was among the final 20. But in the next five years after turning professional he did not manage one League appearance except for a loan period at Swansea City. It was not until moving to Sheffield Wednesday that his career took off

and after spells with Lincoln City, Newport County, Plymouth Argyle and Rotherham United he completed his 200th League goal during his second stint at Plymouth in 1987–88.

England youth international Johnny Skull was on the books of his local club Swindon Town as an amateur when he was offered professional forms. He declined and joined Wolverhampton Wanderers. He did not manage to break into Wolves first team and drifted out of the League to play for Banbury. Seven years after Swindon's first approach they offered him a month's trial in September 1957 which he completed and then signed for them making his Football League debut at last.

Manchester United persuaded Stockport County to allow amateur wing-half Hughie McLenahan to join them in 1927 in exchange for three freezers of ice cream. United scout Louis Rocca arranged for these to be given to the County

club to raise club funds at their bazaar. McLenahan turned professional with United.

Malcolm Shotton was captain of Leicester City reserves when he was axed in 1975. Disillusioned he quit the game and worked as a knitter in a hosiery factory starting work at 6 am. But he was persuaded to return to soccer and played first for Atherstone Town then Nuneaton. Oxford United brought him back to the Football League and in 1986 he captained them in their Milk Cup success over Queen's Park Rangers at Wembley.

At the end of the 1979–80 season Bolton Wanderers goalkeeper David Felgate had reached a total of 61 Football League appearances without playing once in the competition for the club which held his contract. He originally went on loan to Rochdale in October 1978 and made 35 League appearances until the end of that season. In July 1979 he was loaned to Bradford City but made no League

appearances and in September moved on another temporary transfer to Crewe Alexandra, remaining there until January 1980 after 14 appearances in Division Four. In March he returned to Rochdale to add a further 12 League games for the Spotland club.

Injury to Lincoln City's goalkeeper Colin Boulton produced another temporary move for Felgate to the Sincil Bank club in September 1980 but a month later City signed him on a permanent basis. But that was not the end of his loan spells. Four seasons later he made temporary moves to Cardiff City and Grimsby Town.

In July 1953 Bradford City signed Welsh international winger Horace Cumner but he did not make any appearances before moving to Poole Town. On 12 June 1980 Arsenal signed Clive Allen from Queen's Park Rangers and transferred him to Crystal Palace on the 13 August without him kicking a ball in a competitive game.

Gary Goodchild's first six appearances in the Football League were achieved with five different clubs and comprised one full game and five others as a substitute: Arsenal, Hereford United, Sheffield Wednesday (on loan) and Reading before he linked up with Crystal Palace where he added to his senior appearances in 1980–81.

Ian Lawther was transferred from Scunthorpe United to Brentford in the House of Commons on 26 November 1964. The then Brentford chairman Jack Dunnett MP arranged the deal. Dunnett later became chairman of Notts County and then of the Football League.

Gillingham signed Tony Cascarino from Crockenhill in the 1981–82 season in exchange for a set of tracksuits. He went on to become a Republic of Ireland international.

On 7 February 1925, Albert Pape, the Clapton Orient centre-forward, travelled with his side to play against Manchester United in a Division Two match at Old Trafford. Just before the match he was transferred to United, the move being sanctioned by telephone agreement with the Football League. United won 4–2.

NO SHERRY TRIFLE...
After Ipswich Town became a professional club in 1936 their chairman Capt. J. M. Cobbold asked Stanley Rous, then secretary of the Football Association, to recommend a possible manager. Rous reported that Adam Scott Duncan was considered the best in the country. Cobbold decided to drive to Manchester, invited Scott Duncan to return with him to Ipswich whereupon Cobbold telephoned his opposite number at United and told him he was going to appoint Scott Duncan as manager and that he would be sending the United Chairman a case of sherry.

Warney Cresswell was playing for a boys team in South Shields at the age of 13. A team from the opposite bank paid 2s. 6d for the right to play him at centre-half. Yet Benny Fenton might have been considered as the youngest footballer ever involved in a transfer at the age of 12. His Odessa Road school team was disbanded and left him ineligible for West Ham schoolboys. At the time he was their leading scorer. So he was moved to Godwin Road school where the sports master was Vivian Gibbins, former West Ham United and England forward.

Bert Sproston was chosen at right-back for Tottenham Hotspur against Manchester City in a Division Two match at Maine Road on 5 November 1938 and his name was printed on the match programme. But he was then transferred to City and turned out for them against Spurs on the day of the game.

When Port Vale beat Liverpool 4–3 at Vale Park on 8 April 1955, former Liverpool centre-forward Cyril Done scored all four Vale goals in a 4–3 win.

On the day of the transfer deadline on 16 March 1967 Bill Atkins was transferred from Halifax Town to Stockport County with four seconds to go before midnight.

In September 1986 Ian Bennyworth was transferred from Nuneaton Borough to Scarborough in a £1,500 deal. But the player, a 24-year-old travel agent, paid the fee himself in weekly instalments.

In October 1927 Blackpool sent representatives to Nelson to sign Jimmy Hampson. They discovered he had gone to the cinema and persuaded the manager there to flash the following message on the screen: 'Will Jimmy Hampson please call at the manager's office immediately!' He was duly signed there.

DISPLACED PERSONS

These Football League players past and present appear to have played for the wrong teams:

Ken Oxford	Manchester City, Derby County, Chesterfield, Norwich City, Doncaster Rovers, Port Vale
Eric Oldham	Bolton Wanderers, Gateshead, Hartlepool United
Gary Hull	Sheffield Wednesday
Ron Bolton	Bournemouth, Ipswich Town
Jack Charlton	Leeds United
Albert Watford	Chesterfield, Lincoln City
Alan Sunderland	Wolverhampton Wanderers, Arsenal, Ipswich Town
Geoff Bradford	Bristol Rovers
Laurie Sheffield	Bristol Rovers, Newport County, Doncaster Rovers, Norwich City, Rotherham United, Oldham Athletic, Luton Town, Peterborough United
Charlie Birmingham	Everton, Tranmere Rovers
Ronnie Mansfield	Millwall, Southend United.

WINTER WONDER TEAM

Soccer is a winter game as illustrated by these Football League players, past and present:

Arthur Lightening	Nottingham Forest, Coventry City, Middlesbrough
David Raine	Port Vale, Doncaster Rovers, Colchester United
Dave Fogg	Wrexham, Oxford United
Les Blizzard	Queen's Park Rangers, Bournemouth, Orient
Tom Gale	Sheffield

George Snow	Wednesday, York City Wrexham	Derek Showers	Rochdale, Crewe Alexandra Cardiff City,
John Flood	Sheffield United		Portsmouth, Bournemouth,
Billy Hails	Lincoln City, Peterborough United, Northampton Town, Luton Town	Dale Tempest	Hereford United Fulham, Huddersfield Town,
Des Frost	Leeds United, Halifax Town,		Colchester United.

FINAL FARCES

India qualified for the 1950 World Cup finals for the first time but withdrew when they were refused permission to play in bare feet.

Zaire became the first black African nation to reach the World Cup finals in 1974. The country's president promised each player a house of durable quality, a car and a free holiday for their families. All three offers were withdrawn when Zaire lost all its games, failed to score a goal and conceded 14.

A Swedish fan was so incensed by the poor performance of his team in the 1974 World Cup against West Germany that he threw his portable television across the room of his flat. It went through the window and hit the roof of his car parked four storeys below in the street.

Thousands of Italian convicts were able to watch the 1978 World Cup finals in Argentina in the privacy of their cells. Monitor television sets were installed throughout 20 jails in the country 'to avoid the possibility of riots'.

Argentine journalist Osvaldo Ardizzone established a communications record after his team had qualified for the 1966 quarter-finals of the World Cup. His cable to Buenos Aires was 20,246 words long and took 5 hours 40 minutes to transmit.

The original World Cup trophy, the Jules Rimet Trophy, had an interesting life. Hidden under an Italian official's bed in a shoe box to prevent the Nazis stealing it during the Second World War, then stolen in London in 1966 and found

by a dog in a garden suburb, it was presented to Brazil permanently after their third win in 1970. It was stolen again from a display box in Rio de Janeiro and never recovered.

When Northern Ireland reached the finals of the World Cup for the first time in 1958 their Football Association ordered them not to play in two of their three group matches because they were on Sundays. The team ignored the ruling, beat Czechoslovakia and drew with cup-holders West Germany and reached the quarter-finals.

In the 1966 World Cup the opening match between England and Uruguay at Wembley was nearly called off by Hungarian referee Istvan Zsolt when he found that seven England players had left their identity cards in the hotel. A police motor cyclist had to be despatched to retrieve them.

A special World Cup stamp approved by the Post Office and the FA, showing the flags of 16 nations competing in 1966, was banned by the Foreign Office because the government did not recognise North Korea. Hurriedly issued replacements showing footballers in action then became the first British stamps to feature sportsmen.

English referee Jack Taylor, the official in charge of the 1974 World Cup final in West Germany between the host nation and Holland, noticed that all flag-posts in the centre and corners were missing just as he prepared to signal the kick-off. There was a delay while the missing equipment was found.

When the USA trainer ran on to attend to an injured player in the 1930 World Cup semi-final against Argentina, he tripped, fell and broke a bottle of chloroform in his bag. He had to be carried off unconscious while the player recovered without treatment.

The two shortest named players to appear in the World Cup have been Cavetano Re (Paraguay) in 1958 and Francisco Sa (Argentina) in 1974.

In the 1872 FA Cup Final goalscorer M. P. Betts (Wanderers) an Old Harrovian, played under the assumed name of A. H. Chequer because he had once played for Harrow Chequers.

In 1913 Aston Villa's Clem Stephenson revealed that he'd had a dream that Aston Villa would win the FA Cup Final 1-0 with a goal

THE MONSTER MATCH...

In 1934 and 1937 two World Cup qualifying matches involving Hungary and Bulgaria, and Lithuania and Latvia respectively were controlled by Herr Frankenstein of Austria.

headed by Tom Barber. They beat Sunderland exactly like that.

Someone handed Sheffield Wednesday winger Ellis Rimmer a lucky horseshoe at half-time in the 1935 FA Cup Final against West Bromwich Albion. He scored twice in the last five minutes as Wednesday won.

In the 1959 FA Cup Final Roy
Dwight scored for Nottingham
Forest against Luton Town, broke
his leg and watched the second half
on TV from a hospital bed as Forest
won 2-1.

In the dying minutes of the 1956
FA Cup Final, Manchester City
goalkeeper Bert Trautmann broke
his neck but insisted on playing as
City beat Birmingham City 3-1.

In the 1933 FA Cup Final the
players of Everton and Manchester
City were numbered, but from
1-22.

Cardiff City's successful 1927 FA
Cup winning team consisted of one
Englishman, four Irishmen, three
Scots and three Welshmen.
Liverpool's winning team in 1986
had only one player born in
England and he was a Republic of
Ireland international.

Ipswich Town beat Arsenal 1-0 in
the 1978 FA Cup Final. The only
goal came from Roger Osborne in
the 76th minute. It was his last kick
in the match because he had to be
substituted through exhaustion.

When Rangers played Celtic in the
Glasgow Charity Cup in 1930 the
teams were level each with two
goals and four corners which
counted in determining drawn cup
games after extra time. But Rangers
were going off to the United States
for a tour and the cup was decided

by a toss of a coin, which Rangers
won.

When Blackburn Rovers met
Sheffield Wednesday in an FA Cup
semi-final on 6 March 1882, the
game was played at the
Huddersfield Rugby Club ground
because it was the most equi-distant
venue. Goal posts had to be
brought in from Sheffield for the
match, though it did nothing for
Wednesday who, after drawing 0-0,
lost the replay in Manchester 5-1.

Edward Charles Bambridge,
Corinthians and England, suffered a
broken leg some weeks before a
County Cup Final and seemed
certain to miss the game. However
he arrived at the last minute and
changed into his kit. It was
discovered that he was wearing a
white shinguard on one leg. As
these were the days of hacking in
the 1880s, long before the end of
the match it was covered in marks.
Bambridge scored the winning goal
and it was only after the match that
he revealed he had been wearing the
shinguard on his good leg.

Between 1948-49 and 1964-65,
Halifax Town were drawn at home
six times in the FA Cup against non
league opposition: Scunthorpe
United, Ashington, Ashton United,
Rhyl, Burton Albion and South
Liverpool. They did not manage to
win once.

John Anderson, playing for
Manchester United against

Blackpool in the 1948 FA Cup Final at Wembley, hit a surprise shot from 40 yards, fell as he connected with the ball and did not see it enter the net. Neither did Pathe News cameras nor photographers stationed behind the goal.

In 1930–31 during a fourth round FA Cup tie between Southport and Blackpool, a spectator ran onto the pitch only to be tipped back over the railings by players from both sides and the sole policeman on duty at the ground. Southport went on to play Everton in the sixth round and were beaten 9–1. Everton allowed Archie Waterson a goal for Southport and also declined a tenth for themselves when Ted Critchley put the ball into touch in front of an open goal even though he was on a hat trick.